The LONG and WINDING ROAD

A SPIRITUAL GUIDE FOR BABY BOOMERS

Thomas C. Ettinger
and Helen R. Neinast

DIMENSIONS
FOR LIVING

NASHVILLE

THE LONG AND WINDING ROAD: A SPIRITUAL GUIDE FOR BABY BOOMERS

Library of Congress Cataloging-in-Publication Data

Ettinger, Thomas C.
    The long and winding road : a spiritual guide for baby boomers / Thomas C. Ettinger and Helen R. Neinast.
        p.   cm.
    Includes bibliographical references.
    ISBN 0-687-01593-6 (pbk. : alk. paper)
    1. Spiritual life—Christianity.   2. Baby boom generation—Religious life.   I. Neinast, Helen R.   II. Title.
BV4501.2.E856   1998
248.8′4—dc21   98-42482
                                                                                                              CIP

This book was written in partial fulfillment of our Doctor of Ministry degrees in spiritual direction at the Graduate Theological Foundation in Donaldson, Indiana.

Scripture quotations, unless otherwise noted, are from the New Revised Standard Version Bible, copyright © 1989, by the Division of Christian Education of the National Council of the Churches of Christ in the United States of America. Used by permission.

Other quotations are from the Authorized or King James Version of the Bible.

The prayers "My Life Cries Out for You Lord" and "Circle Me Lord" are from *The Edge of Glory: Prayers in the Celtic Tradition,* Copyright © David Adam 1985. Reproduced by permission of Morehouse Publishing, Harrisburg, PA.

The excerpt reprinted from *I Believe in the Resurrection of the Body,* by Rubem Alves, is copyright © 1986 Fortress Press. Used by permission of Augsburg Fortress.

The excerpt from *Meditations of the Heart,* by Howard Thurman, is used by permission of Friends United Press.

Excerpts from *A Way in the World,* by Ernest Boyer Jr., are copyright © 1984 by Ernest Boyer, Jr. Reprinted by permission of HarperCollins Publishers, Inc.

98 99 00 01 02 03 04 05 06 07—10 9 8 7 6 5 4 3 2 1

MANUFACTURED IN THE UNITED STATES OF AMERICA

For our mountain friends

Marty and Jack Haggard
David and Joan Hawthorne
Tom and Maureen Horton
Eva and Chuck Hutton
Lewis and Jeannette Main
Barbara and Don Treanor

people of uncommon grace, especially before a meal

Contents

Introduction

"I think we've been watching too much television," I said. "There's no remedy for that," my grandmother said.
—John Irving, *A Prayer for Owen Meany*

This book is not a "remedy." It is not a self-help book. It is not a self-improvement book. It's not even a self-affirmation book.

This book is simply a companion. It is a companion for those who want to travel a little farther along the "long and winding" road of their lives. It is a companion for those who want to make their way along the path of spirituality.

It is a companion to those of us who are asking, "Is that all there is?" It is a companion to those of us who carry deep anxiety and worry for ourselves, our families, our world. It is a companion for those of us who are worn, wasted, and exhausted, and who would like to find some rest, somewhere, somehow.

It is a book about hope and meaning and endurance and laughter. It is not a book for the fainthearted or for those who are easily distracted. "The spiritual life," as a friend of author Larry Dossey says, "is not for wimps."

The Seventh Veil

In Tom Robbins's novel *Skinny Legs and All*, an Arab and a Jew open a restaurant together across the street from the United Nations. It sounds like the beginning to an ethnic joke, but what follows is both uproariously funny and touchingly poignant. The book's greatest moment comes when the restaurant becomes the venue for an odd showdown between the religious Dance of the Seven Veils and decidedly secular (yet equally religious) Super Bowl. Against this bizarre backdrop, Robbins reveals this truth about spirituality: "Everybody's got to figure it out for themselves." He goes on:

The illusion of the seventh veil was the illusion that you could get somebody else to do it for you. To think for you. To hang on your cross. The priest, the rabbi, the imam, the swami, the philosophical novelist were traffic cops, at best. They might direct you through a busy intersection, but they wouldn't follow you home and park your car.

So, to bend the metaphor a bit, this book is here to help guide you through busy intersections, to point toward crossroads and byways that might be interesting or challenging, to bring your attention to odd signs and road signs, but it is *you* who must do the driving.

Start Where You Are

Pray as you can, not as you can't.
    —Dom Chapman

Responsibility for your own spirituality is a great gift. A Sufi from the twelfth century believed that every human contains the revelation of a different name of God, and thus a different understanding. God reveals Godself in ways unique to each of us. Because of that, each of us has special care for a unique relationship with God and a unique revelation of God.

We are called to pray in ways that make sense to us, that make meaning for us, and that reveal God's presence in the world. That in itself is a tall order. Add to it all the other claims on our lives: careers, relationships, growing children, aging parents, mortgages, and the realities of midlife. There is far too little time in our days as it is, and many of us are too exhausted even to *want* more time.

Yet as a generation of seekers—we seem to have been born to the cause—it is in the end a sense of meaning and a sense of mission for which we long. Tending to that longing gives us life. Tending to that longing gives meaning. Tending to that longing brings with it a sense of mission.

"Spiritual nourishment," Arthur Ashe wrote in a final letter to his daughter, "is as important as physical nourishment, or intellectual nourishment." Sometimes, all three come together in holy moments of knowing who we are and to whom we belong. We are, in truth, children of God.

How to Use This Book

It is a well-known truth that if you read the Gospel story with large glasses on, everything you see will be large. And soon your heart will grow large for looking at big things.
    —Joan Sauro, in *The Kingdom of God Is Like a Circus*

This book is designed to be read with an open mind and an open heart. It is also meant to be *used* with an open mind and heart.

Use this book either by yourself or with a study group. If you are using it on your own, you may want to start at the beginning and work your way through, spending one week with each chapter, or you may want to pick a chapter that seems right for you. The same is true for a study group; you may agree to work through the chapters one by one, or you may decide together week to week what chapter you'll pray with next.

In each chapter, you'll see an opening quotation and scripture, a short reflection, more quotations, a suggested action or spiritual exercise, and a closing prayer.

The opening quotation and scripture are intended to help bring you to focus. The reflection is meant to help you experience some of the richness of the subject at hand. The marginal quotes are there in the hope that they may spark recognition or provoke a smile or take you deeper in your prayer time.

The spiritual exercise is simply a framework for practicing prayer, meditation, and reflection in a focused, sustained way. The spiritual exercises in this book reflect the best traditions of the Christian church, the scriptures, and spiritual seekers around the world. As you practice these exercises, be patient with yourself. Experts (both in psychology and in spiritual direction) say it takes six weeks to establish a new habit—of behavior or of spirituality.

The prayers at the end of the readings are from a variety of sources— the early church, today's writers, ancient mystics, and everyday experience. Pray these prayers as they suit you. You might pray them morning and evening for a while. You could write them on three-by-five-inch cards and carry them in your pocket with you. You might tape them to the refrigerator or the bathroom mirror for a while. Or you could cover an old credit card with white tape, write your prayer on the card, and carry it in your wallet or purse. Whatever form you choose, allow these prayers to be paths to God for you throughout the day.

The Language of Spirituality

Because we are sensitive to inclusive language about people (not using only *he* when the context actually refers to both women and men) and inclusive language for God, we have removed male generic pronouns wherever possible. In places where copyright holders did not give us permission to make changes, we left the original wording. As you read, keep in mind that the authors quoted were often writing without an understanding of our concerns about inclusive language.

Godspeed

From silly devotions
and from sour-faced saints,
good Lord, deliver us.
    —Teresa of Avila

As you wander this road, remember that you are called most of all to be yourself. Tend yourself with grace. Meet yourself exactly where you are, right now, because that is where God will meet you, not with a sour face, but with a kindly one; not with silly devotions, but with the depth and range and surprise of a spirituality that is genuinely, honestly yours.

1

The Spiritual Life

Being Present to the Moment: Mindfulness

"Look, no matter where you live, the biggest defect we human beings have is our shortsightedness. We don't see what we could be."
—Mitch Albom, *Tuesdays with Morrie*

FOCUS

"But the Lord answered her, 'Martha, Martha, you are worried and distracted by many things; there is need of only one thing. Mary has chosen the better part, which will not be taken away from her.'"
—Luke 10:41-42

"See, now is the acceptable time; see, now is the day of salvation!"
—2 Corinthians 6:2

REFLECT

When my younger brother died, my grief was unbearable. I don't remember much of what people said to me at the time; the days before and after his funeral are mostly a blur.

But I do remember a friend who called when she learned of Gary's death. "Oh, God," she said. "Is there anything I can do for you?"

I didn't hesitate. "No. Just come over and be with me."

And that's what she did. She came over and just sat with me. She didn't say anything. She didn't do anything. She was just there, present with me in that terrible, awful time.

"Just to be is a blessing." This traditional Quaker statement of

You are already where you need to be. You need go nowhere else.

—Lawrence Kushner, *God Was in this Place & I, i did not know*

Every aspect of life can be sacred, and each instant, no matter the activity, *can* be holy. Upon the death of his master, Menachem Mendle of Kotzk was asked what had been most important to the teacher whom he had just lost. He thought briefly and replied, "Whatever he was doing at the moment."

—David J. Wolpe, *The Healer of Shattered Hearts*

To look for the good in some other circumstance than the one in which we find ourselves is to trash the only happiness we will ever have: now. Whether it pleases us or not, each moment is a gift.

—Polly Berrien Berends, *Coming to Life*

faith is a simple word about the power of the present, about the power of being present. Whether the moment is one of sorrow or celebration, wonder or mediocrity, it is clear that life happens in the present moment.

When guilt or anger pulls us toward the past, when fears threaten us with the future, when we get too busy or too bored—when this happens, we miss the full richness of life in the present.

Oftentimes we do something so that we may go on to do something else. And because we are focused on what we're going to do *next*, we miss out on what we are doing *now*.

William Shannon quotes a Zen master who said to a pupil, "When you walk, walk. When you eat, eat." The pupil said: "But doesn't everyone do this?" "No," the master said. "Many people, when they walk are only intent on the place to which they are going. They are not really experiencing the walking. They do not even notice they are walking."

Awareness. Presence. Being in the present. Sometimes the noise, the busyness, the demands of our lives crowd out what really matters—not the past, not the future, but the present.

The alternative, of course, is simple and clear: Do one thing at a time. Do it with your whole self. When you eat, eat. When you walk, walk. Give whatever you are doing at the time your full attention, for the kingdom of God, the Bible says, is right here, right now, breaking into this present moment.

ACT

Lectio Divina is one method of prayer used by all traditions of Christian spirituality. This method can be translated as "meditative reading" or "the prayer of the listening heart." Use the scripture from 2 Corinthians above. Read it aloud slowly, pausing between the words. "Savor" the scripture, and try to stay present with it. When a word or thought resonates deeply, sit with it, allowing its fullness to fill your whole being. Perhaps a word or a phrase will capture your attention. There is no need to *do* anything; simply let yourself be in the presence of God and the scripture.

PRAY

O God of peace, who has taught us that in returning and rest we shall be saved, in quietness and in confidence shall be our strength: By the might of thy Spirit lift us, we pray thee, to thy presence, where we may be still and know thou art God.

—Book of Common Prayer

The present moment is significant, not as the bridge between past and future, but by reason of its contents, contents which can fill our emptiness and become ours, if we are capable of receiving them.

—Dag Hammarskjøld

Do one thing at a time, with complete, immediate mindfulness. Don't do it to get it done so you can get on to the next thing. Do it for love. Do it fully, sensitively, openly. Do it now. *Then* do the next thing. Chop wood. Carry water. Type letters. Read mail. Talk to your friend. Bathe the children. Giggle. Fix dinner. Balance the checkbook. Make love. Drink cocoa. Answer the phone. Complain to your boss. Fix the drainpipe. Walk from here to there. Schedule next month's appointment now. Work on the budget. Hammer the nail. Disagree with your colleague. Change the light bulb.

—Gerald May, *The Awakened Heart*

Trust Measured in Inches

FOCUS

"And remember, I am with you always, to the end of the age."
—Matthew 28:20

REFLECT

To trust God with our lives, our whole lives; to offer ourselves, our whole selves, completely to God; to give who we are and who we will be into God's keeping: That is what faith asks of us, but it is a difficult task and a daunting one.

Being called to this level of trust is frightening. It requires much. Perhaps that is why we fill our lives so quickly with all the busyness of living. To trust in God requires a listening heart, and a listening heart requires time. In the face of that requirement, we, not unlike the rich man in Luke's Gospel (18:18-25), turn away from God's call to us with heavy hearts. We have too much to lose by listening to God, by trusting in God, by answering God with our lives.

I have felt often in my life the persistent call of God to trust, and that call has frightened me. If I could control the dynamics of spirituality, trust would be simple, straightforward, and without undue risk. But spirituality does not work that way. Nor does trust. Relationships without the risk of trust are superficial, short-lived, inelegant, unsatisfying.

A day came when God's call to trust evoked in me great desire to respond, but I saw no clear way to do so. In deep spiritual distress, I went out to the countryside for a walk, dropped to the ground, and lay face down in the grass, staring down without seeing. After a few moments, I found myself focusing intently on the ground in front of me. One square inch. My eyes were focused, quite literally, only on what was right in front of my face.

One square inch. A drop of morning dew. A few blades of grass—green, brown, yellow. A small brown twig. Bits of leaves. Red clay soil. A tiny insect slowly making its way across my path.

In that moment, in that place, I began to realize that this one square inch in front of my face held many of life's great mysteries —sunlight and shadow, cells and molecules, atoms and energy. Things seen. Things unseen. Life and death. All of it there—in one square inch.

I realized that I could not begin to understand the intricacies of creation, of life and death, of time's rhythm and flow. If my mind could not grasp the full reality of one square inch of earth, how could I expect to grasp, with my mind, the intricacies of trust between me and God? To place myself in the position of relying on my ability to "understand" as a basis for trust was, in fact, what held me back from trusting God. My trust, at its most basic level, had to be focused not on history, psychology, politics, or the church. My trust had to be focused on the God who created in that square inch of earth more than I could ever fully understand in my entire lifetime.

Since that walk, my prayer life has still been difficult at times. But it has also been joyous. As my trust in God grows stronger, I have been led into a deeper life of prayer. God has shown me new ways of discerning, taught me more about love, and brought me many times to peace in solitude.

Courage comes from the French word *coeur*, which means "heart." In order to travel from clinging to letting go, we have to "take heart."

—Sue Monk Kidd, *When the Heart Waits*

The rabbi was nervously rubbing his free hand across his forehead, as if trying to scratch out a thought. The other hand was clutching a black-bound copy of the Old Testament close to his chest.... "In times like these, Detective, the Word of God brings comfort."

Winter nodded, "And what does He say?"

"He says to trust in His wisdom."

That's what He always says, Simon Winter thought.
—John Katzenbach, *The Shadow Man*

At the same time, God has continued to challenge, confront, and direct me—from within that same context of trust.

How deep, how long, how far will this path of trust in God take me? I do not know. But whenever I get "stuck" I sense God out there ahead of me, encouraging me to trust enough to take the next step. Just one square inch. Just one more step. Just a little more trust.

ACT

Spend some prayer time outdoors. Go for a walk; see what presents itself to you. Listen to the sounds around you. Take time to be still, to study the land and sky around you. How is God's creation revealing itself to you? How does the world around you speak to the issue of trust? Pray with thanksgiving for creation. Pray for trust, for the ability to go one more step with God.

PRAY

And now unto [God] who is able to keep us from falling and lift us from the dark valley of despair to the mountains of hope, from the midnight of desperation to the daybreak of joy; to [God] be power and authority, for ever and ever. Amen.

—Martin Luther King, Jr.

The hardest test I ever faced in my life was praying . . . bending my knees to pray—that act—well, that took me a week. . . . I had to force myself to bend my knees.

—Malcolm X, in Alex Haley, *Autobiography of Malcolm X*

God has not left me alone and will not leave me alone.

—Anne Frank, *The Diary of a Young Girl*

2

Prayer and the Heart's Desire

Deep Communion with God

"God bless you, please, Mrs. Robinson,
Heaven holds a place for those who pray."
—Paul Simon, "Mrs. Robinson"

FOCUS

*"As a deer longs for flowing streams,
so my soul longs for you, O God.
My soul thirsts for God,
for the living God.
When shall I come and behold
the face of God?"*
—Psalm 42:1-2

REFLECT

For Howard Thurman, it was "the hunger of the heart." For John Wesley, it was that moment when he felt "strangely warmed." For Reinhold Niebuhr, it all began in laughter. And for Elizabeth Barrett Browning, it could sometimes be "a gauntlet with a gift in't."

Prayer. A recent edition of *Books in Print* listed nearly two thousand titles on prayer, meditation, and techniques for spiritual growth. That's more than three times the number devoted to sexual fulfillment and how to achieve it.

The desire for intimacy is real, and it is powerful. Prayer is a pathway to spiritual intimacy. Prayer is, quite simply, the heart's deepest desire—the desire for God.

A good way to begin to pray is to begin with yourself—with who you are, right now. Ignatius of Loyola, the sixteenth-century founder of the Jesuits, urged his followers to ask God at the beginning of prayer for what they most wanted and desired. This is the invitation to us to acknowledge our deepest desires and our most immediate needs.

Many of the great Christian teachers use words such as desire, yearning, longing, to describe humanity's search for God. Philip Sheldrake argues for a spirituality of desire in relationship to prayer. This desire and longing is part of who we are as human beings, and it "urges us inward to our center," he writes.

Sheldrake is speaking of *all* our desires—not just the ones that are couched in religious language. We must bring them all to God or else our prayers become prayers of duty and not prayers of love. Sometimes that means we must ask God for the *desire* to desire God, or even, as Ignatius would say, to ask for the *desire to desire to desire* God.

This kind of prayer, at whatever level we begin, leads us deeply inward, so that we begin to discern when the desires of our heart get entangled in the trivial. This kind of prayer guides us surely to our true center, where God waits for us.

Uncover your heart's deep desire. Bring it to prayer. Offer it to God. Let God bless you and make you whole.

I think I know which is God's favorite book of the Bible. I think it has to be the Book of Psalms. In the rest of the Bible, God speaks to us—through seers, sages, and prophets, through the history of the Israelite people. But in the Psalms we speak to [God]. We tell [God] of our love, our needs, our gratitude.
　—Harold Kushner, *Who Needs God?*

People want so much that they do not know.
　—Gwendolyn Brooks, *A Street in Brownsville*

Humor is the prelude to
    faith and
Laughter is the beginning
    of prayer.
—Reinhold Niebuhr, *Discerning
        the Signs of the Times*

She would get on her knees in front of a rickety kitchen chair, grab hold of the edges, holding on for life itself, the way a drowning person grabs hold of a floating board among the flotsam of the sea, and she would pour it all out. . . . I don't think she could have made it without those nightly prayers, which, come to think of it, were more like moanings from the soul's subterranean cells than like words formed by a rational mind.
—Lewis B. Smedes, *Choices*

ACT

One of the earliest formal prayers of the church begins this way:

Almighty God,
to whom all hearts are open,
all desires known,
and from whom no secrets
    are hidden. . . .

Try addressing God this way when you begin your prayers. Pray these words not with fear but with the longing to be known fully.

PRAY

Prayers in the ancient Celtic tradition used repetition as a way to center, focus, and emphasize the desires of the pray-er. This prayer is from David Adam's *The Edge of Glory: Prayers in the Celtic Tradition.*

My life cries out for you Lord
My life cries out for you

My love seeks out for you Lord
My love seeks out for you

My heart yearns for you Lord
My heart yearns for you

My mind thinks of you Lord
My mind thinks of you.

My strength strives for you Lord
My strength strives for you.

THE LONG AND WINDING ROAD

Imagination: Heart and Mind at Prayer

"Captain Robert: These voices of yours. They do not come from God. On
the contrary, they come from your imagination.
Joan: Of course. That is how the messages of God come to us."
—George Bernard Shaw, *Saint Joan: A Chronicle Play in Six Scenes*

FOCUS

*"Then I saw a new heaven and a new earth. . . . And I saw the holy city,
the new Jerusalem, coming down out of heaven from God. . . . And I
heard a loud voice from the throne saying, 'See, the home of God is
among mortals. . . . See, I am making all things new.'"*
—Revelation 21:1-5

REFLECT

The four Gospels, along with a few other sources, sketch some
of the particulars of the life of Jesus—his birth, his baptism, his
ministry, and his passion. But there are many gaps of time, many
of life's passages, that these texts do not address. For these, we
must use our imagination in our attempts to understand what life
was like for Jesus in those times in between Gospel stories.

What does your imagination say about the life of Jesus? How
does your mind's eye picture the growth Jesus experienced in his
life? What does your creativity reflect when you think about
Jesus' childhood, his adolescence, his schooling, his relationship
with his parents?

God has given us this good gift of creative imagination; we use
it with God's blessing and encouragement. When we use it to
imagine Jesus' life more fully, we can be led by God to a better
understanding of Jesus' life and our attempts to respond to Jesus'
life with our own lives. Imagination is a powerful compass on the
path of faith. As the song from the musical *Godspell* says, we are
to see Jesus more clearly, to love Jesus more dearly, and to follow
Jesus more nearly.

Seeking Jesus in this way compels us to use the creative power
of our minds and hearts, of our imagination. Prayer is powerful
when it involves our whole being—intellect, feelings, and the
whimsy of imagination. A life of faithful imagination is a life
open to God, hungry for God, available to God. To commit to
praying with imagination is to fling yourself before God. It is also,

Going to Sunday school can be dangerous, especially if you begin to really believe the things that you are taught.

—Andrew Young, *A Way Out of No Way*

says Frederick Buechner, "perhaps as close as humans get to creating something out of nothing the way God is said to. . . . The highest work of the imagination is to have eyes like [Jesus]."

ACT

The Jesuits have long used imagination in their prayer exercises. Following in that tradition, imagine yourself at the birth of Jesus. Picture yourself there, with all the other attendant people and animals. What does this place look like? How does it smell? How does it feel to be here? Try to use all your senses—touch, smell, sight, hearing, taste.

Imagine who you are and what you are doing at Jesus' birth. What do you see? What is happening? What do you do—help with the birth, sing with the angels, sit shyly alone in a corner, bolt from the scene?

Imagine your feelings. Notice what feelings others around you are experiencing. How do you and they fit into this scene? What does this moment feel like?

Now sit quietly and reflect or write about this prayer experience. God speaks to you through your imagination. What did you hear? What did you learn about yourself? about God? What did you discern?

What gift is God placing before you in this prayer time? Is it consoling, enlightening, challenging, disturbing?

Close your prayer time with an expression of thanksgiving to God. You might speak a prayer of gratitude aloud, or write in your journal. You might take a walk in honor of God's gifts to you, or you might sit quietly and, like Mary, keep all these things in your heart.

She tells him, "You are a son of God, Matthew Poncelet." Visibly touched, he begins to cry, "Nobody ever called me a son of God before. Called me a 'son-of-a-you-know-what' lots of times, but never no son of God."

—Helen Prejean, *Dead Man Walking*

Imagination has always had powers of resurrection that no science can match.

—Ingrid Bengis, "Monroe According to Mailer," *Ms.* (October 1973)

PRAY

Take me, O God.
I surrender myself to you.
In the imagination of my heart, I ask you to draw me close.
In the imagination of my mind, I ask you to guide me this day.
In the imagination of my whole self, I ask you to open my eyes to the wider truth.
In the name of Jesus, this is my prayer. Amen.

3
Giving Yourself to the World

Acts of Kindness

"Like a bridge over troubled water,
I will lay me down."
   —Paul Simon, "Bridge Over Troubled Water"

Focus

"You are the salt of the earth; but if salt has lost its taste, how can its saltiness be restored? It is no longer good for anything, but is thrown out and trampled under foot.

"You are the light of the world. A city built on a hill cannot be hid. No one after lighting a lamp puts it under the bushel basket, but on the lampstand, and it gives light to all in the house. In the same way, let your light shine before others. . . ."

—Matthew 5:13-16

"Then the king will say to those at his right hand, 'Come, you that are blessed by my Father, inherit the kingdom prepared for you from the foundation of the world; for I was hungry and you gave me food, I was thirsty and you gave me something to drink, I was a stranger and you welcomed me, I was naked and you gave me clothing, I was sick and you took care of me, I was in prison and you visited me.'

Then the righteous will answer him, 'Lord, when was it that we saw you hungry and gave you food, or thirsty and gave you something to drink? And when was it that we saw you a stranger and welcomed you, or naked and gave you clothing? And when was it that we saw you sick or in prison and visited you?'

And the king will answer them, 'Truly I tell you, just as you did it to one of the least of these who are members of my family, you did it to me.' "

—Matthew 25:34-40

Reflect

Kent State. The LA riots. Watergate. Drug abuse. Corporate greed. Many of us came of age in a world increasingly marked by cruelty and cynicism.

And in a cruel age, I sing of kindness.

—Aleksandr Pushkin

The world is torn by conflicts, by folly, by hatred. Our task is to cleanse, to illumine, to repair.

—Abraham Joshua Heschel, *God in Search of Man*

Drive-by shootings. Terrorist bombings. Child abuse and homelessness. Our children will come of age in a world that is increasingly hostile and violent.

How do we live in a cruel age? How can we raise children in these troubled times? How can the words of Mahatma Gandhi, Martin Luther King, Jr., Mother Teresa, Nelson Mandela, or Desmond Tutu even begin to address the angers and dangers of our lives today? What is the alternative to despair?

The Jews have a word for it: *tikun olam.* It means "to repair the world." This happens in big ways and in small ones. Sometimes the repair is obvious, noticeable. Sometimes it is quiet, hidden. But it does not happen unless you give yourself to the work of making the world more gentle and just. It does not happen unless you *do something.*

Richard Rhodes, Pulitzer Prize winner for his 1987 book *The Making of the Atomic Bomb,* lost his mother to suicide when he was thirteen months old. When he was ten, his father remarried. Rhodes describes his stepmother being as cruel as the worst of folklore-cruel stepmothers.

For two and a half years, Rhodes and his brother were abused—kicked, beaten, denied baths, deliberately starved. In *A Hole in the World: An American Boyhood*, he writes, "I've often wondered how my brother and I survived with our capacity to love intact. I always come back to the same answer—strangers helped us."

Strangers helped them. Ann Medlock and John Graham, leaders of The Giraffe Project, have made it their life's work to gather and tell the stories of strangers who helped others, who gave themselves to the repair of the world. They call these people giraffes because they "stick their necks out . . . for what they believe in."

Kindness and courage are the touchstones for living a life that gives healing and hope. Sometimes it is hard work to repair the world. Other times it is, as Mother Teresa said, "as simple and as common as the laughter of a child."

ACT

John Wesley believed strongly that Christians are to be about the work of Christ in the world. He wrote: "Do all the good you can, by all the means you can, in all the ways you can, in all the places you can, at all the times you can, to all the people you can, as long as ever you can." Use his words in your morning prayer time to orient you toward your day. Pray

One day we must come to see that peace is not merely a distant goal that we must seek but a means by which we arrive at that goal.

—Martin Luther King, Jr.,
*Where Do We Go from Here:
Chaos or Community?*

. . . The only real hope for creation is for each of us human beings to attend to the yearnings of our hearts so that we can move forward in love instead of retreating or lashing out in fear. If we must sacrifice some of the world's efficiencies in order to find the time and space to do this, so be it.

—Gerald May, *The Awakened Heart*

Faith is not something you must have or cannot lose, but something you practice because the world depends on it.

—Kat Duff, *The Alchemy of Illness*

The growing good of the world is partly dependent on unhistoric acts; and that things are not so ill with you and me as they might have been, is half owing to the number who lived faithfully a hidden life, and rest in unvisited tombs.

—George Eliot, *Middlemarch*

them again in the evening as a way of looking back at the day to discern where and when God is inviting you to help heal the world.

PRAY

Strong covenant God, save us
    from being self-centered in
    our prayers,
    and teach us to remember to
    pray for others.
May we be so bound up in love
    with those for whom we pray
  that we may feel their needs
    as acutely as our own,
    and intercede for them with
    sensitiveness,
  with understanding and with
    imagination.
This we ask in Christ's name.
    Amen.
—Based on words by John Calvin

Resistance as an Act of Faith

"You may say I'm a dreamer
but I'm not the only one."
—John Lennon, "Imagine"

FOCUS

*"Many peoples shall come and say,
'Come, let us go up to the
    mountain of the LORD,
 to the house of the God of Jacob;
that he may teach us his ways
    and that we may walk in his paths.'
For out of Zion shall go forth
    instruction,
 and the word of the LORD from
    Jerusalem.
He shall judge between the nations,
    and shall arbitrate for many
        peoples;
they shall beat their swords into
        plowshares,
 and their spears into pruning
        hooks;
nation shall not lift up sword
    against nation,
 neither shall they learn war any more."*
—Isaiah 2:3-4

REFLECT

Income in America has risen in recent decades, but it's not the poor who have benefited. For example, between 1975 and 1995, the income of America's richest 5 percent grew more than 54 percent, while the poorest 20 percent in our country saw only a 1.5 percent increase.

Discrimination on the basis of race, gender, sexual orientation, and religion continues, showing itself in the workplace, in neighborhoods, and in religious communities. Violence is a fact of life for many of us.

There is nothing harder or less sentimental than Christian realism.
—Flannery O'Connor,
Collected Works

What drove an anonymous Stockholm businessman to leave his safe, neutral country and embark on one of the most perilous missions ever undertaken—wresting Jews marked for deportation from the clutches of Adolf Eichmann and his henchmen?
—Raoul Wallenberg, *Letters and Dispatches, 1924–1944*

You don't have to look very far beyond America's borders to find "ethnic cleansing," mass starvation, and the resurgence of terrorist regimes. Death and dictatorships, rich overclass and poor underclass, malnutrition that kills slowly, and guns that kill with frightening speed, genocide on a mind-numbing scale: How do you give yourself to such a world? What can you do—or even say—in the face of such dire and extreme conditions?

Sidney Harris said that the question "What can one person do?" must be faced by each of us, and that sometimes the answer is this: "One person can do little— but one and one and one and one can do a great deal."

He's right. One and one and one and one *can* do a great deal. As Christians, we are called to be those "one persons." But there is something more needed—something that addresses the sheer *magnitude* of it all.

At the end of her 1992 novel *Possessing the Secret of Joy*, Alice Walker writes of a character being led off to her death. As she passes by, her friends hold up a sign for her. That sign reads, "Resistance is the secret of joy."

Resistance. Not mere survival, but resistance that refuses to die, refuses to lose faith, refuses to let hate win out over love. Walker calls for us to be "in conspiracy" with the divine who seeks justice, mercy, tenderness, and salvation. This salvation is, in effect, a double salvation. As we work with God to save our world, we also work with God to save ourselves. Walker writes of the African American's ancestry of resistance, and we realize it is God's ancestry, too.

ACT

Read the following, one line at a time, and sit with it in prayer. Ask God to help you become more in tune with God's will in this world. Pray this way through the entire creed; allow time for God's spirit to move within you.

PRAY

I go forth into the world
to serve God with gladness;
I will be of good courage,
hold fast to that which is good,
render to no one evil for evil,
strengthen the fainthearted,
support the weak,
help the afflicted,
honor all people,
love and serve God,
and rejoice in the power of the Holy Spirit.
—Adapted from *Services of the Church #1*, United Church Press

So, let us be alert—alert in a twofold sense: Since Auschwitz we know what [we] are capable of. And since Hiroshima we know what is at stake.
—Viktor E. Frankl, *Man's Search for Meaning*

Bread for myself is a material question; bread for my neighbor is a spiritual question.
—Nikolai Berdyaev, *The Fate of Man in the Modern World*

There is no story more moving to me personally than one in which one woman saves the life of another, and saves herself, and slays whatever dragon has appeared.
—Alice Walker, *Living by the Word*

4

A Spirituality of Honesty

Sin, Confession, and Repentance

"I'm trying to tell you something about my life
Maybe give me insight between black and white."
—Emily Saliers of the Indigo Girls,
"Closer to Fine"

FOCUS

"Incline your ear, O LORD, and answer me,
for I am poor and needy. . . .
Teach me your way, O LORD,
that I may walk in your truth;
give me an undivided heart to revere your name. . . .
For great is your steadfast love toward me;
you have delivered my soul
from the depths of Sheol."

—*Psalm 86:1, 11, 13*

REFLECT

Sin. Confession. Repentance. Even though I'm at middle age, the images that come to mind when I hear those three words are images from my childhood.

"Now I lay me down to sleep. I pray the Lord my soul to keep. If I should die before I wake, I pray the Lord my soul to take." As a child, there were no words more frightening than these spoken at bedtime. What if I *did* die in the night? Would God take my soul to heaven, or would the unkind words and fights I'd had with my brothers force God to abandon both me *and* my soul, just when I needed God most?

It was frightening for me as a child; it remains frightening for me, still, some nights, as an adult. I don't worry, now, so much about dying in the middle of the night and being found wanting. I worry instead about *waking* in the middle of the night and being "found out."

I find it hard to be honest about who I am. About who I *really* am. With myself, with other people, with God—I'm afraid of the truth about who I am. Confession is out of the question; repentance is surreptitious and shadowy; to ask for forgiveness requires too much courage.

Yet the longing, the yearning, to be fully known—and still loved—is strong. Oftentimes the urgency drives me to distraction; sometimes it drives me to my knees, to risk it all. All that I am—the good, the bad, the beautiful, the ugly, the wondrous, the awful—all that I am tumbles out in a rushed heap before God.

And God gently gathers all of it in outstretched arms, gathers all of me to God's breast, and speaks softly the power of love's forgiveness. I rest, at least, in the peace of being fully known . . . and fully loved.

ACT

Elizabeth J. Canham in her article "Homecoming" writes this: "In the past, catalogues of sins to check before going to confession were sometimes offered. But such lists can shortcut our responsibility to

The soul is frail, but God is full of compassion for the distress of the soul, for the failure of the heart.

—Abraham Joshua Heschel,
God in Search of Man

H. R. Mackintosh, a Scottish theologian, says that the process of forgiveness is first owning and then disowning our sins.

—Doris Donnelly, *Learning to Forgive*

Private prayer allows us the time . . . to think about ourselves and know ourselves better . . . to turn over the stones in our souls and see what lives under them.

—Gertrud Mueller Nelson,
To Dance with God

It is but natural that we expose to Thee the things in us that seem most worthy and good. . . . But deep within us we know that this is not enough. We know that somehow we must be totally exposed to Thee. . . . Teach us to know that Thy love is so whole and so healing that nothing less than all of us can rise to meet Thine all-encompassing care.

—Howard Thurman,
Meditations of the Heart

Even Judas could not escape. He hanged himself. But tradition tells us that Jesus "descended into hell." This time it must have been Jesus who kissed Judas, repeating the same words as in the garden: "Friend, why are you here?" But this time they were a resurrection invitation to Judas: "Follow me." Jesus knows the way out, even out of hell. Together they walked, and all of creation walked with them, through the Red Sea to death's other side.

—W. Paul Jones, *The Triduum*

wait upon God with the prayer: 'Search me, O God, and know my heart; test me and know my thoughts. See if there is any wicked way in me, and lead me in the way everlasting' (Psalm 139:23-24)."

She goes on to assert that God, always eager to forgive, is always calling us to conversion and then giving us the power to live and to change.

Sit quietly with these verses from Psalm 139 and ask God to speak to you through them.

PRAY

God help us to find our confession:
The truth within us which is hidden
    from our mind . . .
The stowaway which has been
    smuggled
Into the dark side of the heart,
Which puts the heart off balance and
    causes it pain. . . .
Lead us into the darkness that we
    may find what lies concealed;
That we may confess it towards the
    light;
That we may carry our truth in the
    centre of our heart;
That we may carry our cross wisely
And bring harmony into our life and
    our world.
Amen.

—Michael Leunig

(Michael Leunig is a newspaper cartoonist whose work regularly appears in Melbourne, Australia's *Age*. In the early 1990s, he also began writing prayers for publication in this newspaper.)

Cynicism

"When the President does it, that means that it is not illegal."
—Richard Nixon, interview with David Frost

"Therefore, since we are justified by faith, we have peace with God through our Lord Jesus Christ, through whom we have obtained access to this grace in which we stand; and we boast in our hope of sharing the glory of God. And not only that, but we also boast in our sufferings, knowing that suffering produces endurance, and endurance produces character, and character produces hope, and hope does not disappoint us." —Romans 5:1-5

REFLECT

There are some passages of scripture that irritate me. This is one of them. From childhood through adolescence, and on into my adulthood, I have been unable to appreciate this word from Paul to the Romans. There's been enough suffering, for God's sake. Enough endurance. Far too much "character-building." And too little reason for hope.

Generally speaking, we are cynical people. We're critical—hypercritical. We're pessimistic. We're all too familiar with malaise, negativity, and defeatism. Sarcasm and satire, a sharp-toothed unkindness, are second nature.

Watergate. The My Lai massacre. Iran-Contra. The Tuskegee Experiment. Madison Avenue's seductive promises. Clinton and Starr.

It's no wonder that we are cynical. The world, the country, and our own families have given us ample opportunities to learn the art of finely honed cynicism. Bob Dylan says it well: "You don't need a weatherman to know which way the wind blows."

Cynicism is an ill wind, and one that shipwrecks many of us. Whether it's the long, sustained damage of constant disappointment, or the sudden devastation of intimate betrayal, we are all wounded. The cost is our lives, our ideals, our spontaneity, our relationships, our creativity, and our imagination. Cynicism deadens the soul, as surely as bitterness and pessimism wear it out.

Politics these days is not so much a movie as an endless reel of cotton-candy coming attractions. When, I wonder, will my generation—the generation of Clinton and Blair—have its own rendezvous with destiny?
—Walter Shapiro in *USA Today*
(May 2, 1997)

I worry no matter how cynical you become, it's never enough to keep up.
—Jane Wagner, *The Search for Signs of Intelligent Life in the Universe*

Jesus struggled with cynicism and with disillusionment and with despair. He knew anger and never tried to hide or suppress or sublimate it. Instead, he claimed it and cared for it.

He used humor—not the biting satire that makes you feel worse, but the bright wit that acknowledges life's frequent absurdities. He sought companionship—from colleagues, family, and friends who refused to deny the day's harsh betrayals, but who also refused to ignore them. He sought refuge in faith—in prayers and worship that bring all the anger and cynicism before a God who is humorous, companionable, and faithful beyond belief.

Be strong. Stay focused. Know that in the face of cynicism, faith has the last word. And that word—heard as laughter, felt as friendship, known through faith—is hope.

ACT

The ancient Celts in their prayer time would sometimes draw a circle around themselves, symbolizing God's encircling presence. Draw a circle around yourself clockwise, either with your index finger or in your mind. Feel the encircling power and protection of God, and know that you are in God's care. As you pray, you might want to recite the following Celtic prayer. Or you might recite some other prayer of protection and hope. Practicing an awareness of the presence of God is a powerful way to address cynicism and to evoke hope.

PRAY

Circle me Lord
Keep protection near
And danger afar

Circle me Lord
Keep hope within
Keep doubt without

Circle me Lord
Keep light near
And darkness afar

Circle me Lord
Keep peace within
Keep evil out.

—David Adam, *The Edge of Glory: Prayers in the Celtic Tradition*

Cynicism is an unpleasant way of saying the truth.
—Lillian Hellman, *The Little Foxes*

The world is full of people who have lost faith; politicians who have lost faith in politics, social workers who have lost faith in social work, schoolteachers who have lost faith in teaching and, for all I know, policemen who have lost faith in policing and poets who have lost faith in poetry. It's a condition of faith that it gets lost from time to time, or at least mislaid.
—P. D. James, *A Taste for Death*

5

Spirituality and Work

Making Meaning

"The alarm clock shrieks, and you drag yourself out of bed, jump in the shower, jump out, wake and dress the kids, pour the cornflakes, grab last night's homework, start the car, stop at the day-care center, fight the traffic, and arrive at your desk, already dazed by the day's demands. From there on, it's a whirl of errands, details, and deadlines—on the job and back at home—which finally winds down about 15 minutes before you do. Sitting down in front of the tube or picking up that new novel you've been looking forward to all evening, you're soon snoring. Another day, another case of exhaustion."

—Jay Walljasper in *Utne Reader* (July-August 1991)

FOCUS

"For you, O LORD, have made me glad by your work; at the works of your hands I sing for joy."

—Psalm 92:4

REFLECT

The Yankelovich Monitor, an annual survey of social values, has for several years asked a representative sample of working women what would get them to stop working permanently. The number of women who said that having enough money would get them to stop was 35 percent in 1987. By 1990, that number had jumped to 56 percent. In another survey of working men, the number who described their job as a career dropped to 48 percent in 1990.

We have become disenchanted with work many times in past history. The sweatshops of John Wesley's day were oppressive, dangerous, and soul-numbing. Henry David Thoreau wrote of the wealthy as terribly impoverished. Thirty years ago, many young people turned their backs on formal society, switched to whole grain foods, and left the city for the country. (Most have since returned, in one way or another.)

Is work a blessing or a curse? Sometimes it's hard to tell the difference. Work as job, work as career, work as calling—the categories and labels get confusing, and confused, in the course of the demands of daily life.

Work, according to Genesis, is not meant to be dehumanizing, oppressive, or exhausting. Adam and Eve are expected to till and to keep the garden, but the expectation is not an unhealthy one. "Work," says Doris Donnelly, "even in paradise, is part of human fulfillment."

How did we stray so far from work-as-pleasure to work-as-punishment? The answer is part sociology—a consumer culture, an economics based on the illusion of affluence—and part spirituality, the idolatry that what we do determines the value of who we are.

And so what is to be done in the face of all this? How do we recover meaning and moderation in our work? How do we manage to make a living while we pay attention to making a life?

The pitcher cries for water to carry
and a person for work that is real.
—Marge Piercy, *To Be of Use*

Q: So you're happier when you're working.
A: Yes, it's an important distraction.
—Woody Allen, in a "Rolling Stone" interview

I think that most of my fatigue is related not to the type of work I do but to the false tensions I put into it. If I could just live the day quietly, obedient to the order of the day . . . then my mind would be more vacant for God and freer for all the simple things of every moment.

—Henri J. M. Nouwen,
Genesee Diary

Our vocation is not a sphinx's riddle, which we must solve in one guess or else perish. Some people find, in the end, that they have made many wrong guesses and that their paradoxical vocation is to go through life guessing wrong. It takes them a long time to find out that they are happier that way.

—Thomas Merton, *No Man Is An Island*

The key to discovering answers to these questions lies in exploring work as a path to God. Work has both an exterior and an interior character—the exterior character of tools, knowledge, and skills; and the interior character of creativity and inventiveness. The dailiness of work is precisely the place where an intentional Christian lives out her or his vocation. There is a big difference between trying to bring God to one's work and seeing God already at work there.

Jean Blomquist writes about her struggle to recover balance and meaning in her work:

The yearning to create . . . lodges deep in the human heart. . . . Perhaps that is why we feel so frustrated and unfulfilled when our work seems to inhibit rather than express our deep gladness. . . . It may help us to remember that, as in the Beginning, the creativity of work often takes place in the darkness and emptiness. . . . As we seek to mend relationships, negotiate conflicts, discover direction or meaning, discern whether to stay in a job or to leave, we enter a sacred space where we learn more about ourselves, others, and God.

ACT

As you seek to recover, or discover, meaning in your work, take some time to think about these suggestions from "Discovering Our Deep Gladness: The Healing Power of Work," an article by Jean Blomquist: "Observe your life carefully, closely, and reverently. What gives you energy, joy, satisfaction? To what do you devote yourself fully and freely? Be attentive, especially in difficult situations. What might it mean to choose life here?" And remember this: Discovering your call, your work is not a luxury. According to Blomquist, it is a necessity.

PRAY

'Tis the gift to be simple,
'Tis the gift to be free,
'Tis the gift to come down
Where we ought to be.
And when we find ourselves
In the place just right,
'Twill be in the valley
Of love and delight.
                —Traditional (Shaker)

One must not always think so much about what one should do, but rather what one should be. Our works do not ennoble us; but we must ennoble our works.
—Meister Eckhart, *Work and Being*

Your Money or Your Life

"Do not buy stuff you cannot afford, unless you really want to."
—Winston Groom, *Forest Gump*

Focus

"But if we have food and clothing, we will be content with these. But those who want to be rich fall into temptation and are trapped by many senseless and harmful desires that plunge people into ruin and destruction. For the love of money is a root of all kinds of evil, and in their eagerness to be rich some have wandered away from the faith and pierced themselves with many pains."

—1 Timothy 6:8-10

Reflect

Schwinn bicycles. Hot Wheels. Lava lamps. Bass Weejuns. Hush Puppies. Nehru jackets. Barbie dolls. GI Joe. Model airplane kits. VW Beetles. Record albums. Eight-track tape players. McDonald's. Superman.

Long before we grew up to become adults earning salaries, we learned how to spend money. It was Etch-a-Sketches and Tootsie Rolls then; now it's Toshiba laptops and Ben & Jerry's "Chubby Hubby" ice cream.

So we earn money, and we spend it. We earn more; we spend more—and spend and spend and spend . . . you get the idea.

Acquiring things, getting into debt, working harder—or longer—to get more money to get out of debt: it's a bone-wearying circle, even when your income approaches six figures.

We Americans have such conflicted notions about money. We believe that money means freedom and security; yet no matter what our income most of us also believe that if we only earned twice as much, we'd be happy and secure. No other country spends a higher percentage of its income, or saves a lower percentage.

Most people find it difficult to tell someone exactly what they make because they believe at bottom that they are worth only what they earn. It's a strange, disorienting idolatry.

Our attitudes about money and our attachment to it are complicated by our personal family histories, our culture's free-spending habits, our deeply ingrained bent toward consuming, and our own levels of spending. Consumerism is an easy target for condemnation, but coming to terms with money and things as spiritual "commodities" is infinitely harder.

Jacob Needleman says that "the challenge of our life is to face the money question without disappearing into it or running away from it." Time given to the pursuit of money is time taken away from other things in life—being with family, reading for pleasure, hiking in the woods, thinking and reflection.

How much money is enough? What kind of security does money provide? Does making money always mean impinging on those who live "below" us economically? What responsibilities does earning money bestow on us?

John Kavanaugh in *Still Following Christ in a Consumer Society* writes that the real threat in all this is not necessarily material things and possessions, but the idolatry of them. The problem is not technology, but worship of it. The problem isn't even capitalism, he says, but its enthronement as a "way of life...which suffocates persons and personal values."

How can we get beneath these and other questions to find some way to think about money that will help us provide for our families *and* be more faithful to God? Maybe it will help to remember that Jesus calls us to live both joyfully *and* responsibly in our financial relationships. We can also

Lord, won't you buy me a Mercedes Benz.
My friends all drive Porsches, I must make amends.

—Janis Joplin

By poverty is meant enough to live on.

—Virginia Woolf

Things filled [people] with fear: the more things they had, the more they had to fear. Things had a way of riveting themselves onto the soul and telling the soul what to do.

—Bruce Chatwin,
The Songlines

keep in prayer the reality that the pursuit of wealth leads us away from ourselves, from our center. And we must realize that if money is something we choose to trade our life energy for, we must make our choices about that trade with reverence and care.

ACT

"Most clutter enters our lives through the 'more is better' door. It comes from the disease of materialism, of looking for inner fulfillment in outer possessions." This assertion by Joe Dominguez and Vicki Robin in *Your Money or Your Life* resonates quite well with the Hebrew and Christian scriptures. Money is important; after all, we must support our families. But money, in itself, and the things it can buy, are a dead end.

Focus in your prayer time on the places in your life that are cluttered. Do you have too much "stuff"? Is your credit overextended? Do you live from one paycheck to the next, nagged by anxiety and worry? How comfortable are you with where you and your family are financially right now?

God promises to guide us when we bring ourselves in prayer, asking for direction and help. Meditate prayerfully on your money and your life. In prayer, examine your material possessions. Study the amount of time you devote to making a living. Listen for what God might be calling you to do with your finances, with your possessions, and with your vocational gifts.

PRAY

Dear Lord, you are the Truth. When I keep myself rooted in you, I will live in the Truth. Help me, Lord, to live a truthful life, a life in which I am guided not by popularity, public opinion, current fashion or convenient formulations but by a knowledge that comes from knowing you. . . . Lord, bring me always closer to you who are my teacher, always teaching me out of love. Amen.

—Henri J. M. Nouwen, *A Cry for Mercy: Prayers from the Genesee*

The argument is for a lifestyle that allows people to have enough, but not so much that it damages their own lives, others' lives, and the life of the planet.

—Cecile Andrews, *The Circle of Simplicity*

Each human being must participate. That is the wisdom in the Jewish law mandating that the first thing a beggar must do, upon receiving charity, is donate a portion to another more needy than he.

—David J. Wolpe, *The Healer of Shattered Hearts*

Intimacy with God

Spirituality and Our Bodies

"In the dying days of the 20th century we humans have an increasingly strange relationship with our physical selves. Obsessed by our bodies—with what we put into them, how well muscled they are, how efficiently they work—we are at the same time growing more estranged from them."

—Lynette Lamb, *Your Body: Friend, Foe, or Total Stranger?*

FOCUS

"Do you not know that your body is a temple of the Holy Spirit within you, which you have from God, and that you are not your own? For you were bought with a price; therefore glorify God in your body."
—*1 Corinthians 6:19-20*

REFLECT

In *The Human Body Shop*, Andrew Kimbrell writes that "we have declared war on our bodies." The newest body battleground, he says, is our increasing preoccupation with body image.

Whether it is body image, destructive work habits, or the habitual abuse and misuse of our bodies, this most intimate environment—the human body—is the one we are most aggressively exploiting in the escalating war against the body. Whether through neglect, self-destruction, or narcissism, we have sacrificed our birthright from God.

As Christians, we still give lip-service to the sacredness of the body, but our prevailing perspective and actions have turned the body secular and, at times, even profane. Rubem Alves says it well: "The doctrine of the incarnation whispers to us . . . that God, eternally wants a body like ours." But, he goes on to say, a strange temptation happened to us, and we started to look for God in perverse places. We thought we'd find God where the body *ends*, and so we turned our bodies, and the bodies of others, into beasts of burden, labor-producers, slaves to fashion and form, and soon the smell of death—not life—surrounded the body.

The humanity of God, as well as our own humanity, disturbs us. But it does not have to be so. We can leave the smell of the tomb. We can delight in the wonders of paradise. And we can do that now. We can pray for our bodies—for peace, for reconciliation, for pleasure. We can also pray *with* our bodies—our hands, our feet, our walking and running and dancing.

According to our sacred tradition, our bodies are the temple of the Holy Spirit. That means that we—our bodies—are bearers of the Spirit, and that we must live in our bodies in ways that allow the Spirit to be embodied there.

ACT

In *Prayer and Our Bodies*, Flora Slosson Wuellner makes several good suggestions for allowing our bodies to become full spiritual partners in our praying. Color is an energizing focus for prayer. Touching a flower or a stone, washing your face and hands with

The body is not destined to be elevated to spirit. It is the Spirit which chooses to make itself visible, in the body.

—Rubem Alves, *I Believe in the Resurrection of the Body*

Incarnation means that God finds us, and we find God, in the human faces of one another and in the human fabric of our lives.
—Diana L. Eck, *Encountering God: A Spiritual Journey from Bozeman to Banaras*

Prayer with open eyes and open palms, meals which are consciously savoured, addresses to which people can react with shouts, clapping or even whistling, the kiss of peace, music which not only touches the ears but moves the body, dance which expresses religious experiences and relationships with others, are promising beginnings of a new church which is again finding its way back to human embodiment.
—Elisabeth Moltmann-Wendel, *I Am My Body*

running water, listening to the sound of your own breathing, sitting on the ground and keeping silence—these ways of praying encourage the whole body to be present. Walking, in itself, can be a prayer. Wuellner suggests taking a "parable walk," in which you set out with no special agenda but simply ask God to show you something that will be meaningful or relevant to you. You may, she says, find comfort, insight, or renewal. Try one—or more—of these suggestions to enrich your prayer time.

PRAY

As the body is clothed in cloth
and the muscles in the skin
and the bones in the muscles
and the heart in the chest,

So are we, body and soul,
clothed in the Goodness of God
and enclosed.
God is the means
whereby our Substance
and our Sensuality
are kept together
so as to never be apart.
　　　　　　　—Julian of Norwich

Conflict in Relationships

"Of all the worn, smudged, dog's eared words in our vocabulary, 'love' is surely the grubbiest, smelliest, slimiest. Bawled from a million pulpits, lasciviously crooned through hundreds of millions of loud-speakers, it has become an outrage to good taste and decent feeling, an obscenity which one hesitates to pronounce, for, after all, Love is the last word."
—Aldous Huxley, "Adonis and the Alphabet"

FOCUS

"My God, my God, why have you
forsaken me?
Why are you so far from helping
me, from the words of my groaning?
O my God, I cry by day, but you do
not answer;
and by night, but find no rest."
—Psalm 22:1-2

"The LORD is my shepherd, I shall
not want.
He makes me lie down in green
pastures;
he leads me beside still waters;
he restores my soul.
He leads me in right paths for his
name's sake."
—Psalm 23:1-3

REFLECT

I have sometimes found myself desolate, hurt, and angry with God. I have sometimes found myself consoled, taken care of, and trusting in God.

"My God, my God, why have you forsaken me?"

"The Lord is my shepherd, I shall not want."

I remember the first time it dawned on me that these two psalms, back-to-back in the Bible, capture so much of what is human about us. I began to wonder if David, the reported author of these psalms, felt at times about God the way I do. Was it possible that, with three thousand years between us, David and I each could feel both forsaken *and* cared for?

For the sanity of friend-ship, and the madness of love, Thanks be to the Lord, Our God.

—A. S. T. Fisher,
Fellows' chaplain,
Magdalen College, Oxford

How is it that we can move from feeling forsaken to feeling beloved, even intimate, with God? I think the road between the two is partially paved with the resolution of the conflict.

That's true between us and God—we must get angry and tell God how we feel. We must name the conflict. That gives God and me something to work with in prayer and reflection. It gives us a chance to work our way back toward center. Conflict, and the resolution of conflict, makes me more intimate with God—be-cause it makes me more honest with God, and, I believe, lets God be honest with me.

The willingness to resolve con-flict is the very stuff that intimacy is made of. This is true in relation-ship to God; Jesus is a good exam-ple of that. The Gospels report that Jesus felt challenged by God (in the wilderness), pushed emotionally by God (in the Gethsemane gar-den), forsaken by God (on the cross). Yet, there was resolution of these feelings, an end to the con-flict, an intimacy between the two.

The same thing is true for our relationships with other people. The dullest, most life-draining relationships we have are those in which there is no honest dia-logue, no straightforward state-ment of problems, no direct dealing with conflict. Intimacy comes only when conflict is

THE LONG AND WINDING ROAD

faced, talked about, and re-solved in some manner. A "good argument" results in the inti-macy of honesty, vulnerability, and risk.

This is what God wants—both between God and us, and between us and our mate, our family, our friends. God yearns for intimacy with us and wants our intimacy with others to grow. It takes courage to risk intimacy. It takes energy. It takes prayer. But exam-ples of that courage and that ener-gy are all around us—in the Bible, in the example of Jesus, in our close friends and family.

In ways we do not fully understand, self-disclosure helps us to see things, feel things, imagine things, hope for things that we could never have thought possible.

—Alan Loy McGinnis, *The Friendship Factor*

ACT

John Veltri, a Jesuit priest in Canada, offers this adaptation of the "Blessed History" exercise.

Our own personal history, made up of so many diverse expe-riences, becomes blessed when, after sufficient remembering and listening with the heart, we begin to discover God present and working with us through all of it. The following is a way of opening oneself to this constant presence of God in one's life for reflection and analysis.

1. Begin by remembering the sig-nificant persons, events, and experiences in your life. You might list these chronologically or in segments of three years or by association. Then, draw a hori-

As soon as you notice the slightest sign of indifference, the moment you become aware of the loss of a certain seriousness, of longing, of enthusiasm and zest, take it as a warning. You should realize your soul suffers if you live superficially.

—Albert Schweitzer, *The Search for Meaning*

zontal line across a sheet of paper and divide it into three-year or five-year segments. Chart your life experiences on this line.

2. Look at all these events, and begin to note the gifts God has strewn in your path. Make connections between different events and the meanings they have for you.

3. Reflect in prayer with God on some of these significant events and experiences. Try to see God's presence and to understand it. Gradually try to see that God has been constantly present with you, not only in isolated, separate moments of time but continuously as companion, friend, lover, guide.

4. As you close this exercise, ask God for the grace to see and appreciate God's presence in your life.

PRAY

Lord, my God, when Your love
    spilled over into creation,
You thought of me.
    I am from love . . . of love . . . for love.
Let my heart, O God, always recog-
    nize and enjoy your goodness
    through all creation.
Direct all that is in me toward your
    praise.
Teach me reverence for every person
    and all living things.
Energize me in your service.
Lord God, may nothing ever distract
    me from Your love,
    neither faith nor fear

health nor sickness
wealth nor poverty
honor nor dishonor
long life nor short.
May I never seek nor choose to be
   other than
what You yearn for me to be.
   Amen.

—Ignatius of Loyola, *Principle and
   Foundation*, adapted by
   Thomas C. Ettinger

I had a lover's quarrel with
the world.

—Robert Frost, epitaph

7

Family Life as Spiritual Discipline

Making and Keeping Commitments

"The toughest job in the world isn't being President. It's being a parent."
—President Bill Clinton, 1994

Focus

"For this reason I bow my knees before [God], from whom every family in heaven and on earth takes its name. I pray that . . . you may be strengthened in your inner being with power through [the] Spirit, and that Christ may dwell in your hearts through faith, as you are being rooted and grounded in love." —*Ephesians 3:14-17*

Reflect

According to Thomas Wolfe, you can't go home again. According to most of my therapy group, who'd want to? Ogden Nash says it tongue-in-cheek in his poem "Family Court," but for some of us it's true:

> One would be in less danger
> From the wiles of the stranger
> If one's own kin and kith
> Were more fun to be with.

It's hackneyed, but true: Close to half of all marriages in America end in divorce. One of the many institutions that faltered in the seventies was the traditional nuclear family. Divorce doubled, marriages dropped off, and by 1976 only 7 percent of American families bore any resemblance to the Cleavers. What's more, the number of people choosing to live alone rose by 60 percent.

While we looked to TV—*The Brady Bunch, The Waltons, Happy Days*—for a sense of belonging to a family, we often felt estranged from our own. Add to that *All in the Family, The Jeffersons,* and *The Mary Tyler Moore Show* (no children, no spouse, but creating family around her nevertheless), which depicted something a little closer to reality, the mix becomes even more confusing.

As we have put our own families together as adults—committing to a partner, raising children, opening family life to friends and community—we have found the way fraught with danger. Commitments—to ourselves, to our partners, to our children, to our friends—are hard to make and even harder to keep, not because we are morally weak or hopelessly selfish, but because our culture fragments relationships.

We must make our workplaces and work schedules more humane. We must teach our children (and ourselves) to honor child-rearing as much as career-building. We must build communities where work and play and hearth-keeping can be shared.

In the meantime, our relationships *can* be salvaged. Spiritual disciplines such as honesty, compassion, reflection, and prayer build good relationships. So does accepting the challenges as well as the joys that come with family life.

Home is where one starts from.
—T. S. Eliot, *The Four Quartets*

Home is the place where,
  when you have to go there,
They have to take you in.
  —Robert Frost, "The Death of the Hired Hand"

And there are many among us who have *never* known a real home: orphans, perhaps, or those whose habitations were so filled with strife and loneliness that they didn't come near the meaning of the word "home." Whether or not we have actually been without a home, there is within each of us something of the homeless one, the exile . . .
—Betsy Caprio and Thomas M. Hedberg, *Coming Home*

There is a special dynamic in hard creative work alongside someone you are in love with. The ideas flow differently, and there is a common vividness.

—Mary Catherine Bateson,
Composing a Life

I had a chance to talk with [my mother], one of those conversations where you're not 100 percent certain you're going to see the person again. In talking to her . . . I saw her strength: her belief that life is always good, no matter how hard it is, that living your life with honor has great value and pursuing life with courage is always worthwhile.

—Ron Howard, *A Nice Guy
and a Winner*

ACT

Sit in prayer by yourself and think about each member of your family. Picture them—their faces, their dispositions—in your imagination. The time you spend on this exercise is not as important as just doing it. You may spend more time on one family member than another; you may include extended family or "chosen" family—friends who have become family to you. You may even wish to include prayers for family you have lost to death. Say the family member's name to yourself. Repeat the name. Imagine God's arms surrounding him or her. Be reflective and listen. This exercise will almost always heighten your sensitivity and compassion for those you care about so much.

PRAY

Accept, O God, my thanks and praise for all that you have done for me and my family. For those things that are unresolved or painful among us, I ask your help. I thank you for the blessing of family and friends, and for the loving care that encompasses us on every side. As we have been loved by others, we ask you for the chance to share our family's love with others—those alone, cast out, lonely. Grant us the gift of your Spirit, that we may know you and make you known in all the works of our hands. Amen.

Is There Childcare in the Desert?

"Sometimes when the twins are sleeping I look down at them and I feel this rush of tenderness and I am amazed at the love I feel. And *then* they wake up!"
—Jane Wagner, *The Search for Signs of Intelligent Life in the Universe*

FOCUS

"Then Jesus said, 'There was a man who had two sons. The younger of them said to his father, "Father, give me the share of the property that will belong to me." So he divided his property between them. A few days later the younger son gathered all he had and traveled to a distant country, and there he squandered his property in dissolute living. When he had spent everything, a severe famine took place throughout that country, and he began to be in need. So he went and hired himself out to one of the citizens of that country, who sent him to his fields to feed the pigs. He would gladly have filled himself with the pods that the pigs were eating; and no one gave him anything. But when he came to himself he said, "How many of my father's hired hands have bread enough and to spare, but here I am dying of hunger! I will get up and go to my father."'"

—Luke 15:11-18a

REFLECT

As Ernest Boyer listened to a talk at Harvard Divinity School on the spirituality of the desert, he felt himself drawn to the life of solitude and prayer. He also felt frustrated. As a husband and father of three small children, he wondered whether the commitments of the desert could be reconciled with his commitments to his family.

He approached the lecturer as she was putting away her notes and said, "Just one question. Is there childcare in the desert?"

For those of us who share life with a partner, with children, or with grandchildren, this is no small matter. Exhausted by the daily demands of working—on the job and in the home—paying the bills, cooking meals, fixing school lunches, mending hurt knees, refereeing disagreements, tending to our relationships with our children and our mate, we often despair of finding time for ourselves *or* for God.

In an attempt to answer these questions for himself, Boyer wrote *A Way in the World: Family Life as Spiritual Discipline*. He

Cruel blows of fate call for extreme kindness in the family circle.

—Dodie Smith, *I Capture the Castle*

My children cause me the most exquisite suffering of which I have any experience. It is the suffering of ambivalence: the murderous alternation between bitter resentment and raw-edged nerves, and blissful gratification and tenderness.

—Adrienne Rich, *Of Woman Born*

calls family life "the sacrament of the care of others and the sacrament of the routine." Work done for love is a prayer, an act of worship, a special devotion. He says these things not out of some bleary-eyed romanticism, but from the rigors of the day-to-day life of his own family. (The Desert Mothers and Fathers faced their own day-to-day rigors, and came to the conclusion that prayer is work and work is prayer.)

Still, the question remains: How does one attend to the life of reflection while simultaneously attending to one's life as a parent? In one of the last chapters of his book, Boyer gives five "rules" for bringing the two ways of life—solitude and family—together. While he is quick to point out that these rules do not make the job easy, he suggests they do make it possible.

Taken from his book, Boyer's rules are:

1. *Balance Time.*
Lack of time is of course the central problem. The life of care of others is one that consumes every moment of the day. How is it possible to find more time for the self-creation of life on the edge? The answer is that it is not possible to find *more* time, but it is possible to find *some* time. . . . Have a pre-arranged minimum length for it (it may be as little as twenty minutes) in a period of the day when you are least likely to be disturbed and most able to make

THE LONG AND WINDING ROAD

good use of the time. . . . Whenever it is, whatever its length, stick to it.

2. *Arrange Space.*

Everyone trying to join the life of self-creation with that of care needs a space all their own within the home, one set apart as much as possible, a place to withdraw. For those lucky enough, this might be a separate room all their own. For others it might be a desk they alone use or perhaps only a comfortable chair in a quiet corner of the bedroom.

3. *Keep Close.*

Keeping close is simply that process of making the extra effort to reach out to those whose life you share. Sharing the same rooms and seeing each other day after day does not in itself draw people together.

4. *Rituals of Separation and Return.*

For many, the word "ritual" conjures up images of elaborate ceremonies, of incense and music. I am thinking of something much simpler, little gestures really, but gestures that come to remind family members of their ties to one another and that point to their efforts to stay close to one another even in situations where they may have to be separated for brief periods. . . . A little ritual of separation and return that small children especially enjoy is the exchanging of small personal items to be safeguarded during an absence. A child might give a small toy or a stone she found, the parent a tie clip or ribbon. Each keeps what he or she was given until the parent returns; then they give them back again.

5. *Living Off Balance.*

The final rule for joining the life of the desert with that of the family is remembering that the union is seldom

We do our best for our children, never knowing for sure if it is enough or if we are doing it correctly. This is courage.

Marilyn Martone, *What Families Can Teach*

a smooth one. . . . You feel yourself an inhabitant of two worlds, but a citizen of neither. . . . The task now is to learn to accept this imbalance, to see in it a sign of all that is being attempted. And perhaps with practice there may come a time when the imbalance can be steadied, the halting, stumbling gait smoothed and evenly paced and so transformed into dance, a lifelong dance that makes a home for a family and a place in the desert.

ACT

Look over Boyer's five "rules" for combining solitude and family life. Note which of these you are doing well, and which need your attention. Do not try to make several changes in your life at once; live your way slowly into them so that you can make your way through to your own rules.

The love that I had for my daughter was lost in the anxiety I had for my daughter. The only way I knew to be a father was to take care of her, as my father had been unable to take care of me, to move heaven and earth if necessary to make her well [Buechner's daughter was suffering from anorexia], and of course I couldn't do that. I didn't have either the wisdom or the power to make her well. . . . The best I could do as her father was to stand back and give her that freedom even at the risk of her using it to choose for death instead of life.

—Frederick Buechner, *The Dwarves in the Stable*

PRAY

God grant me the serenity to accept the things I cannot change;
courage to change the things I can;
and wisdom to know the difference.
Living one day at a time; enjoying one moment at a time;
accepting hardship as the pathway to peace;
Taking, as Jesus did, this sinful world as it is, not as I would have it;
Trusting that our Loving God will make all things right if I surrender to God's will;
That I may be reasonably happy in this life,
and supremely happy with our Caring God forever in the next. Amen.

—Reinhold Niebuhr (attributed)

The parable of the prodigal son is a story that speaks about a love that existed before any rejection was possible and that will still be there after all rejections have taken place. It is the first and everlasting love of a God who is Father as well as Mother. It is the fountain of all true human love, even the most limited.

—Henri J. M. Nouwen, *The Return of the Prodigal Son: A Story of Homecoming*

Trust yourself: You know more than you think you do.

—Benjamin Spock and Stephen J. Parker, *Dr. Spock's Baby and Child Care Book*

8

Hopes, Wishes, Dreams

Change: Chaos, Choices, Hope

"Future shock. . . . the shattering stress and disorientation that we include in individuals by subjecting them to too much change in too short a time."

—Alvin Toffler, *Future Shock*

FOCUS

"For in hope we were saved. Now hope that is seen is not hope. For who hopes for what is seen?"

—*Romans 8:24*

REFLECT

Tolstoy once defined hell as being deprived of choices. But for me, in my life, hell at times has been being *confronted* with choices. I hate change. I despise choices. Forget the road not taken—just leave me be on my familiar, well-worn path. That's my honest feeling, most days. But when I face life head-on (or, rather, when life faces *me* head-on), I know that, at the core, change truly is my constant companion. It's the one thing I can count on. My unfailing attendant. My ever-present reminder that I am not completely in charge of it all.

So I find transition times hard. I get anxious when I lose hold of the familiar and stumble across the strange. I'm ill at ease moving from home territory to an unfamiliar continent. It's sometimes hard even to move from the routine of unhappiness to the risk of happiness—at least the sadness was *familiar.*

THE LONG AND WINDING ROAD

As I'm dragged, kicking and screaming, through one transition or another, I stubbornly drag hope along with me. Hope that I'll see it through to the other side. Hope that there *is* another side. Hope that the pain—or the joy—will not be too much to bear. Hope that I'll manage some grace, or that some grace will manage me, in the process.

ACT

Julian of Norwich was thirty years old and at death's door when she received her "showings" or revelations from God in May of 1373. Forty-three years later, this English mystic was still working to understand the mystery of her visions. The following prayer is one of those revelations she struggled throughout her life to understand. As you pray Julian's prayer, ask for guidance and understanding, a revelation of your own.

PRAY

I may make all things well, and I can make all things well, and I shall make all things well, and you will see yourself that every kind of thing shall be well.
—Julian of Norwich, *Showings*

There are many incidents which can eviscerate the stalwart and bring the mighty down. In order to survive, the ample soul needs refreshments and reminders daily of its right to be and to be wherever it finds itself.
—Maya Angelou, *Wouldn't Take Nothing for My Journey Now*

Every one of us is called upon, probably many times, to start a new life. A frightening diagnosis, a marriage, a move, loss of a job or a limb or a loved one, a graduation, bringing a new baby home: it's impossible to think at first how this all will be possible. Eventually, what moves it all forward is the subterranean ebb and flow of being alive among the living.
—Barbara Kingsolver, *High Tide in Tucson*

When Reuben left, it did not crush her. It was no longer a desertion, merely a parting. She could survive in peace. She packed away her thick dresses and shoes, she stacked her books—and with a light heart, two suitcases, and a ticket to Botswana, prepared to take leave of her past.
—Carolyn Slaughter, *Dreams of the Kalahari*

Discerning God's Will in
Your Life

"People are always going out west to find themselves. In the seventies they went to California. Now they seem to be finding themselves in New Mexico. I have a cousin who found herself in Santa Fe a few years ago. She just wasn't happy in Georgia."
—Bailey White, *Mama Makes Up Her Mind and Other Dangers of Southern Living*

FOCUS

"Rejoice in the Lord always; again I will say, Rejoice. Let your gentleness be known to everyone. The Lord is near. Do not worry about anything, but in everything by prayer and supplication with thanksgiving let your requests be made known to God. . . . Finally, beloved, whatever is true, whatever is honorable, whatever is just, whatever is pure, whatever is pleasing, whatever is commendable, if there is any excellence and if there is anything worthy of praise, think about these things."

—Philippians 4:4-6, 8

REFLECT

God's will: That's a slippery subject, depending on where you are and with whom you're discussing it.

"He was so young, but God called him home. His death must be God's will," someone says. So a child is buried, dead at age nine, and his parents are left to ache with unasked questions.

"Manifest Destiny is God's will," someone argues. "It makes America complete, from sea to shining sea." No mention here of the Native Americans who already were living on this continent and were being slaughtered by war and disease.

And what of God's will in this new millennium? There are innumerable people out there willing to tell the world what God wants—and most of it is power politics masquerading as religion.

Is it possible to discern the will of God—for society, for your family, for yourself? It is possible, but the process of discernment may take you places you never imagined.

Discernment begins with a deeper definition of God's will. In the Bible, when you see the word *will* in relation to God, it is more accurately translated "yearning." God's will is God's *yearning* for us. So the question becomes, "What does God yearn for us?"

To begin with, God's will, God's yearning for us, is not an impersonal blueprint forced on us. God, says Gerard W. Hughes, wants us to "discover what we really want and who we really are." In Hughes' words, "God's will is our freedom."

That freedom leads us down a path of discernment—to find out, as Frederick Buechner put it, "where our greatest joy and the world's deepest need meet"; to find out what we need to do, because God is not finished with the world and needs our help; to find out what our gifts are; to listen to the counsel of those whom we respect and love; to find out what it means to pay attention to our hopes and dreams and to discern how they fit in with our lives; to offer it all to God in prayer, and to listen for God's yearning for us.

This is what it means to seek God's will. It is a holy call to discern God's yearnings and our yearnings. Pay attention: The path of discern-

For all that has been—
  Thanks!
For all that shall be—Yes!
    —Dag Hammarskjøld

Each of the major choices [in my life] was accompanied by a great deal of anxiety and torment: seeking, searching, questioning, and worrying. . . . Looking back over the years, patterns emerge and one learns, with difficulty, to discern the hand of God in one's daily existence. The will of God even becomes something we learn to look for and to pray for.

—Andrew Young, *A Way Out of No Way*

ment is covered with prayer, courage, trust, and creativity.

Act

The process of discernment begins with a question—a specific question that has to do with change and decision making, such as something to do with work, relationships, career changes, family, money, and so forth.

Use the following for discernment.

1. What is your bias, preference, or desire going into this discernment process? Try this exercise to help clarify your thinking. Take a sheet of paper and make two columns. Head one column "I will accept this new job opportunity." Above the other, write "I will not accept this new job opportunity." Then, under each column, make two subcolumns which read "advantages" and "disadvantages." Spend some time considering each of these two options, and list the advantages and disadvantages of each. Use this as information as you proceed with the discernment process.

2. Spend time in prayer laying out before God the decision to be made, asking specifically

for help in understanding and discerning God's will for you. Listen. Just spend time listening.

3. You may want to ask a few people you love and respect for their opinions and viewpoints.

4. Take an objective look at what you have learned and gathered from this process. Note what God may be trying to tell you. Offer it to God and ask for confirmation. If you don't feel you have confirmation, start the process over again.

PRAY

My Lord God, I have no idea where I
  am going.
I do not see the road ahead of me.
I cannot know for certain where it
  will end.
Nor do I really know myself, and the
  fact that I think that I am following
  your will does not mean that I am
  actually doing so.
But I believe that the desire to please
  you does in fact please you.
And I hope that I have that desire in
  all that I am doing.
I hope that I will never do anything
  apart from that desire.
And I know that if I do this you will
  lead me by the right road though I
  may know nothing about it.
Therefore will I trust you always
  though I may seem to be lost and in
  the shadow of death.
I will not fear, for you are ever with

The snail does the Holy Will of God slowly.
—G. K. Chesterton (attributed)

I suspect we are all recipients of cosmic love notes. Messages, omens, voices, cries, revelations, and appeals are homogenized into each day's events.

—Sam Keen, *The Passionate Life*

me, and will never leave me to face my perils alone.

—Thomas Merton

9

Ritual, Symbol, Sacrament

Marking Time as Holy

"Ritual is food to the spiritually hungry."
—Letty Cottin Pogrebin, *Deborah, Golda and Me*

FOCUS

"Moses was keeping the flock of his father-in-law Jethro, the priest of Midian; he led his flock beyond the wilderness, and came to Horeb, the mountain of God. There the angel of the LORD appeared to him in a flame of fire out of a bush; he looked, and the bush was blazing, yet it was not consumed. Then Moses said, 'I must turn aside and look at this great sight, and see why the bush is not burned up.' When the LORD saw that he had turned aside to see, God called to him out of the bush, 'Moses, Moses!' And he said, 'Here I am.' Then he said, 'Come no closer! Remove the sandals from your feet, for the place on which you are standing is holy ground.'"

—Exodus 3:1-5

REFLECT

Patterns. Rhythms. Reminders of life's constancy.

Moments. Pauses. Interruptions. Reminders of life's dissonance.

These are the things that rituals mark. Ceremonies. Graduations. Celebrations. Funerals. Prayers at mealtimes. The nightly routine of going to bed and the daily routine of getting up. The mundane constancy of Moses' life—tending his father-in-law's flock every day—interrupted by the unexpected and the miraculous: a burning bush that marks God's sudden appearance.

"From beginning to end," writes Robert Fulghum, "the rituals

The word *symbol,* of Greek origin, literally means "something that pulls together...." Bread is a symbol of nourishment, of Jesus, of the gift of salvation, of the church.... Wine symbolizes joy, conviviality, life, and suffering. In the eating of this holy food believers are nourished by Jesus.

—Mark P. Bangert, *Symbols and Terms of the Church*

of our lives shape each hour, day, and year. Everyone leads a ritualized life: rituals are repeated patterns of meaningful acts. If you are mindful of your actions, you will see the ritual patterns. If you see the patterns, you may understand them. If you understand them, you may enrich them. In this way, the habits of a lifetime become sacred."

For a friend of mine with two young daughters, the ritual of getting each of them settled into her bed for sleep each night is sacred, warm, and holy. Bedtime stories, books read aloud, goodnight kisses, and sleepy murmurings of "I love you, Mom" mark this time as nothing else can.

For those of us who can remember exactly where we were and what we were doing when we first heard that JFK had been assassinated, the state funeral that followed was a service of high ritual for a shocked and horrified society. The public murder of a president was so numbing that we—as a nation and as individuals—desperately needed ritual to help get us through those first awful days and weeks.

As creatures of rhythm, we, no less than the rest of creation, are captured by rituals. Great ones and small ones. Daily ones and once-in-a-lifetime ones. In many ways, our basic needs for living are extraordinarily simple, and they haven't changed much over

THE LONG AND WINDING ROAD

the centuries. We eat, sleep, bathe, work. Understanding and creating rituals in these areas of life can enrich our everyday acts.

Jesus himself had a fine sense of ritual. In his teaching, in his daily life with his followers, at meal-times, at the beginning and the ending of the day—he blessed these times by understanding the power of the moment and honoring it with a ritual. And his followers, to this day, never forgot him for it.

ACT

Saint Benedict structured the day around what he called the Divine Office, or the Opus Dei, the Work of God. Eight times a day the Benedictines gathered to offer praise to God. The basic structure was this:

Vigils: before dawn
Lauds: at daybreak
Prime: about 6:00 A.M.
Terce: about 9:00 A.M.
Sext: about noon
None: about 3:00 P.M.
Vespers: dusk
Compline: before bed

You might think about applying some portion of Benedict's office in your life. Lunchtime, midday, may be a good time to stop and mark the day with prayer and reflection. Or perhaps morning or bedtime is a better choice for you. Whatever time you choose, use

The human spirit loves rituals. Rituals connect us to wonder, to self-discovery, to the world of myths and symbols.

—Jennifer Louden, *The Woman's Comfort Book*

"Rituals" is my term for patterns you create in your everyday living that uplift the way you do ordinary things.

—Alexandra Stoddard, *Living a Beautiful Life*

Ritual affirms the common patterns, the values, the shared joys, risks, sorrows, and changes that bind a community together. It helps us face together those things that are too painful to face alone.

—Starhawk, *Ritual to Build Community*

the Benedictine format of hymn (read or sung), psalm, scripture reading, and prayer. Try this discipline for one month.

PRAY

The last verse of Saint Patrick's hymn reminds us of the rhythm of God's abiding presence with us. Pray it as part of your daily rituals—a reminder of life's holiness.

Christ be with me, Christ within me,
Christ behind me, Christ before me,
Christ beside me, Christ to win me,
Christ to comfort and restore me,
Christ beneath me, Christ above me,
Christ in quiet, Christ in danger,
Christ in hearts of all that love me,
Christ in mouth of friend and
    stranger.

Making Time for Worship

"And the people bowed and prayed
to the neon God they'd made."

—Paul Simon, "The Sound of Silence"

"Day by day, as they spent much time together in the temple, they broke bread at home and ate their food with glad and generous hearts, praising God and having the goodwill of all the people. And day by day the Lord added to their number those who were being saved."

—Acts 2:46-47

"For where two or three are gathered in my name, I am there among them."

—Matthew 18:20

REFLECT

The kids' Sunday morning soccer games; an eight-inch-thick Sunday morning paper; waffles, fresh-squeezed orange juice, and a leisurely Sunday morning breakfast; cable television with dozens of shows on dozens of stations: These—plus so many other things, like late-night Saturday soirees and innumerable household chores and the thought of Monday's return to a hectic work week—are the things that keep us from the nourishment our souls crave.

Weekly worship: Marking time by making time to be part of a faith community. Most worship services are still held on Sunday mornings, but many churches have Saturday evening services, midweek services, and daily mass. As inconsequential as it might seem at first, gathering weekly for worship is one of the most crucial disciplines of the spiritual life.

We don't come to worship to "find God." We come, rather, to be found by God. It is only in community that we discover who we really are.

Jewish law prefers that Jews pray together rather than alone, and we Christians are heir to that bias. Joseph Telushkin, author of the "Rabbi Daniel Winter" murder mysteries and a leader of the National Jewish Center for Learning and Leadership, writes, "The rabbis apparently felt that public prayers are more apt to be offered for that which benefits the entire community, whereas individuals often pray for that which benefits only themselves."

In a world in which any moments of rest, celebration, meditation—the festivals of any religious tradition or spiritual orientation—are often seen as a "waste of time" [we must see that] there is joy in our very decision to join in noting them, in celebrating them, in walking the spiritual path—the spiral—that they make.

—Arthur Waskow, *Seasons of Our Joy*

The greeting and singing, the reading, the telling, the praying, the offering, blessing, breaking, pouring out, and receiving always point to what God will yet do with us. . . . All liturgical gatherings . . . are pregnant with the future.

—Don Saliers, *Worship as Theology*

Dan Wakefield, writing about his own spiritual journey, realized that going to church, even belonging to a church, did not solve his life's problems. Rather, he writes, "It gave me a sense of living in a larger context, of being part of something greater than what I could see through the tunnel vision of my own personal concerns."

Henri Nouwen, in an interview shortly before his death, said that he had discovered that community worship was crucial for his prayer life. "I can do prayer best when I do it in the company of others," he said.

As an antidote to spiritual myopia, as a place to be found by God, as a call to something greater, worship is critical to your ability to discern who you are and what you're called to do.

It is true, of course, that all faith communities have their frailties, their off days, their unpalatable members. As Evelyn Underhill wrote, "The Church is an 'essential service' like the Post Office, but there will always be some narrow, irritating and inadequate officials behind the counter and you will always be tempted to exasperation by them."

Don't let soccer games, or Sunday chores, or irritating individuals keep you from worship. Communion with God and with other believers is too vital, too central to who you are.

ACT

When you go to worship next, commit yourself to a deepening presence in the service. Pay prayerful attention to the scriptures that are read, the hymns that are sung, the prayers of petition and thanksgiving that are offered. Pray for the worship leaders. Pray for your participation in the service. Listen to the service with your heart. What is God trying to say to you in this time of worship? In the following week, see what you recall most vividly from the service. Try in one sentence to recall the scripture passage and the message of the sermon. Pray for those who were named in the prayers of intercession, and for those you know who are in need. Do you remember the hymns that were sung—either words or tunes? What about your interactions with people who were at worship with you? Spend some time reflecting on all this.

You may want to do this again when you go to worship next week. See if it helps your preparation and focus in worship.

PRAY

Today, today, today. Bless us . . . and help us to grow.
　　　　　—Rosh Hashanah liturgy

Every [one] lives in two realms, the internal and the external. The internal is that realm of spiritual ends expressed in art, literature, morals, and religion. The external is that complex of devices, techniques, mechanisms and instrumentalities by means of which we live. Our problem today is that we have allowed the internal to become lost in the external.
　　　　　—Martin Luther King, Jr.,
　　　　　Where Do We Go From Here:
　　　　　Chaos or Community

Together with the whole people of God, with people from all over the world, you are invited to live a life exceeding all your hopes. On your own, how could you ever experience the radiance of God's presence?
　　　　　—Brother Roger of Taize

10

Solitude, Rest, Sabbath

Balance and Rhythm

"Time is on my side, yes it is."
—Meade and Norman of the Rolling Stones, "Time Is On My Side"

"The soul has its own sense of time and its own odd forms of clock and calendar."

—Thomas Moore

FOCUS

"For everything there is a season, and a time for every matter under heaven:
  a time to be born, and a time to die;
  a time to plant, and a time to pluck up what is planted;
  a time to kill, and a time to heal;
  a time to break down, and a time to build up;
  a time to weep, and a time to laugh;
  a time to mourn, and a time to dance;
  a time to throw away stones, and a time to gather stones together;
  a time to embrace, and a time to refrain from embracing;
  a time to seek, and a time to lose;
  a time to keep, and a time to throw away;
  a time to tear, and a time to sew;
  a time to keep silence, and a time to speak;
  a time to love, and a time to hate;
  a time for war, and a time for peace."

—*Ecclesiastes 3:1-8*

REFLECT

Kathleen Norris writes in *The Cloister Walk* about her changing relationship with time. While our culture often sees time as a commodity in too short supply, or an enemy that "chews us up and spits us out with appalling ease," Norris tells of a friend who says she owes to the Benedictines her sanity regarding time: Time from a monastic perspective is most readily seen as a gift. Norris's friend says, "You never really finish anything in life . . . and while that's humbling, and frustrating, it's all right. The Benedictines, more than any other people I know, insist that there is time in each day for prayer, for work, for study, and for play."

Time.

Time in each day.

Time in each day for prayer, for work, for study, and for play.

Time, lived in the firm belief that there can be—indeed, that there is—rhythm and balance in each day of life. This is no "cloistered fantasy" of monks with endless days and no responsibilities; it is a blessing of nature to which we are all beckoned to return.

Everything in this world moves in rhythm. Scientists affirm the rhythm of the solar system despite the planets' sometime tendency toward creative chaos. Reclaiming balance and rhythm is perhaps our most challenging spiritual quest.

To bring ourselves—body, soul, mind, strength—to center is, in a deep and powerful sense, to remember who we are. It is to remember *whose* we are; our God

Just to be is a blessing. Just to live is holy.

—Abraham Joshua Heschel, *I Asked for Wonder*

It is not a question of stopping the movement of life; it is a question of fulfilling it.

—Simone de Beauvoir, *The Ethics of Ambiguity*

Many women, like myself, wrestle with a tyrannical perfectionism that insists that every task be completed—every dish washed and letter answered—before sitting down to rest, or write, or do whatever it is that gives us pleasure.

—Kat Duff, *The Alchemy of Illness*

Ignoring our seasons of the spirit can also be a source of stress. There are times when it feels natural to be active and out-flowing, and there are times when it feels natural to be more indwelling and contemplative. If we consistently expect the same level of spiritual, emotional, and physical activity of ourselves, we are headed for trouble.

—Flora Slosson Wuellner, *Prayer and Our Bodies*

created us for joy, for wisdom, for happiness, for wholeness.

There are hundreds of books that teach techniques for managing life and time. But reclaiming balance is not about technique. It's about approach—approaching life as it is meant to be. It's about seeing—seeing all of life as a piece of one fabric. It's about valuing—valuing life enough to live it freely.

The admonition "take time to be holy" is in fact an invitation to take time simply to be: to be rested, to be creative, to be whole, to be in rhythm with God.

We know how anxiety-producing it is to be chained and bound by time. We know how restful it is to fall into rhythm and balance. "We are," writes Jeremy Rifkin in *Time Wars*, "at a critical point when we must decide which sort of time we will embrace—linear or rhythmic, manic or balanced, stunted or sacred."

ACT

Howard Thurman, pastor, philosopher, and educator, has been called "one of the greatest spiritual resources of this nation." Born in a segregated town in 1900, his spirituality of hope and reconciliation has had a far-reaching impact on leaders in America and around the world. Use the following excerpt from *Meditations of the Heart*, one of more than twenty books Thurman wrote before his death in 1981, in a time of reflective journaling and prayer. Respond to the questions raised. Conclude by asking God to help you find some balance in your day.

PRAY

How good it is to center down!
To sit quietly and see one's self
    pass by!
The streets of our minds seethe
    with endless traffic;
Our spirits resound with clash-
    ings, with noisy silences,
While something deep within
    hungers and thirsts for the still
    moment and the resting lull.
With full intensity we seek, ere the
    quiet passes, a fresh sense of
    order in our living;
A direction, a strong sure purpose
    that will structure our confu-
    sion and bring meaning in our
    chaos.
We look at ourselves in this wait-
    ing moment—the kinds of peo-
    ple we are.
The questions persist: what are we
    doing with our lives?—what
    are the motives that order our
    days?
What is the end of our doings?
    Where are we trying to go?
Where do we put the emphasis and
    where are our values focused?
For what end do we make sacri-
    fices? Where is my treasure
    and what do I love most in life?
What do I hate most in life and to
    what am I true?

I have taken time off. Literally. The watch that straps my workaday wrist to its demands sits on the kitchen shelf.

I have shed its manufactured time, its minute hand, hour hand, just the way I shed my city wardrobe.... Gradually, I have even begun to lose track of time. First the minute and then the hour, finally the day. My watch and I have wound down.

—Ellen Goodman, *Making Sense*

May you treasure wisely
this jeweled, gilded time
And cherish each day as an
extra grace.

—Andrew Greeley, *Irish
American Blessings and
Prayers*

Over and over the questions beat in
upon the waiting moment.
As we listen, floating up through
all the jangling echoes of our
turbulence, there is a sound of
another kind—
A deeper note which only the stillness of the heart makes clear.
It moves directly to the core of our
being. Our questions are
answered,
Our spirits refreshed, and we move
back into the traffic of our
daily round
With the peace of the Eternal in our
step.
How good it is to center down!

The Noble Art of Leaving Things Undone

"To sit alone on a quiet night—to invite the moon and tell her one's sorrow—to keep alone on a good night—and to call the insects and tell them one's regrets."

—Lin Yutang, *The Importance of Living*

"Come to me, all you that are weary and are carrying heavy burdens, and I will give you rest. Take my yoke upon you, and learn from me; for I am gentle and humble in heart, and you will find rest for your souls. For my yoke is easy, and my burden is light."

—Matthew 11:28-30

Reflect

Even God rested. It says so in the Bible. Farmers let fields lie fallow from time to time. School lets out for the summer (in most communities, at least). Major league baseball takes a three-day All-Star break midseason. And the industrious ant returns to its cool, dark underground home each evening.

Not so for us. We live with—demand, actually—twenty-four-hour stores, day-and-night automatic banking, and the relentless speed of the Internet.

"The three great American vices," says Chinese scholar Lin Yutang, "seem to be efficiency, punctuality and the desire for achievement and success. They are the things that make Americans so unhappy and so nervous." He goes on to speak of the inalienable right to loaf: he talks about the noble art of getting things done and the nobler art of leaving things undone.

Jesus, who was much in demand and besieged by a great number of people, managed to do two things. First, he taught great multitudes, but he met those in need one person at a time. Second, he went away by himself, prayed, spent time in quiet, and rested.

In *A Life We Never Dared Hope For*, Brother Roger of the Taize community in France instructs believers to "rest your heart in God, let yourself float on the safe waters." Thomas Keating, a Trappist monk, says that the goal of centering, restful prayer is "not to relax us in ways we may achieve with yoga, deep breathing, or jogging, but to allow us to rest in God by uncovering an intimacy that reveals our true selves."

Time for them was a wonderful thing.... They had no phobia about the idleness of sitting still, they saw no point in doing a thing too quickly, just to rush on to the next. There was always more time; one should use it leisurely.

—Carolyn Slaughter, *Dreams of the Kalahari*

Every person needs to take one day away.... On [my] getaway day I try for amnesia. I do not want to know my name, where I live, or how many dire responsibilities rest on my shoulders.

—Maya Angelou, *Wouldn't Take Nothing for My Journey Now*

Stillness. Quiet. Rest. Sabbath solitude. These are the ways we let go of all the plans and purposes of our lives so that we grow closer to the God who dwells in us. Jesus went to the temple, to the desert, to the mountains, to his home. Hear his plea for Sabbath keeping. Leave things undone. Rest—not out of exhaustion, but out of joy. Play—with no purpose other than enjoyment. Lie in bed a little later in the morning, and when you do get up, get up more slowly.

ACT

Do nothing. For fifteen minutes one day, simply do nothing. Leave something undone, and do nothing. If you catch yourself starting to do something, put it away and go back to doing nothing. Sometimes, it's time to "do nothing" for God.

PRAY

Reflect on this poem before entering into a time of prayer.

why hills are draped
in blankets of cicada-song
book-toting two year olds climb willing
    laps
and sheep graze
a winding choreography
to the barn

why whippoorwill begins her seam-
    less chant
and winds renounce the ceaseless
push and pull, become

as cool fingers
beneath a collar

why evening porches,
Duluth to Galveston, bend
rhythmically to the hymnody of
rocking chairs
and slowly swaying calves

because the tune of twilight
is Sabbath.
—Doug Hitt, "Adagio"

You cannot pour from an empty cup. A weary body cannot serve itself, much less someone else.
—Judith L. Boice, *The Art of Daily Activism*

Prayer begins where expression ends.
—Abraham Joshua Heschel, *Man's Quest for God*

11

Mortality, Change, Loss

On Losing One's Youth

"And now my life has changed in oh so many ways,
My independence seems to vanish in the haze."

—John Lennon and Paul McCartney, "Help!"

FOCUS

"For it was you who formed my inward parts;
    you knit me together in my mother's womb.
I praise you, for I am fearfully and wonderfully made.
    Wonderful are your works;
that I know very well.
    My frame was not hidden from you,
when I was being made in secret,
    intricately woven in the depths of the earth."

—Psalm 139:13-15

REFLECT

It has happened. You wake up one morning, find your body's a little stiff, and think how nice it would be to lie in bed awhile longer. You've gained a few pounds, and you're finding it harder to lose them. You've begun to have trouble reading the menu at restaurants. And you realize that the music your adolescents worship isn't all that appealing—in fact, you can't even understand the lyrics.

It happens. Like it or not, we are actually aging. It is not, for most of us, a graceful process. We are not, in our eyes, a pretty sight. We are determined, quite vigorously determined, not to go gently into that dark night.

Yet, as Stephen Levine writes in *Who Dies?*, "Observing the body's decay, the change in metabolism as we age, the graying at the temples, the middle-age paunch, the lowering of energy levels—the lessening of muscle tone, the loss of hair—how can we deny the temporariness of the body?"

Mortality, change, loss. Our body's betrayal of us—it seems maudlin to dwell on these things. But it is the acknowledgment of our impermanence that frees us at last to live. Embracing change allows us to live in the present. Honoring the aging process lets us live into the future. Respecting death strengthens our enthusiasm for living.

None of this is easy, of course. The death of innocence, of memory, of beloved friend or parent—these deaths are companioned by anger and grief. So we who strive to live by faith know what poet Ann Weems knows about grief and loss: "There is no salvation [for our grief and anger] in self-help books; the help we need is far beyond self. Our only hope is to march ourselves to the throne of God and in loud lament cry out the pain that lives within our souls."

Lament. Throw rocks. Stomp around. Shout. Curse. Cry. Laugh at your own frailty, and at the absurdities of aging. And do all this before the throne of God.

Strange how when you're young you have no memories. Then one day you wake up and, *boom*, memories overpower all else in your life.

—Douglas Coupland, *Polaroids from the Dead*

I think when you pass forty you automatically start thinking about your own mortality.

—Jane Fonda, *Los Angeles Weekly* (interview, 1980)

Blessed are those who mourn, for they will be comforted.

—Matthew 5:4

As we reach midlife in the middle thirties or early forties, we become susceptible to the idea of our own perishability....It is a paradox that as we reach our prime, we also see there is a place where it finishes.

—Gail Sheehy, *Passages*

I have occasionally had the exquisite thrill of putting my finger on a little capsule of truth, and heard it give the faint squeak of mortality under my pressure.

—E. B. White, Letter to Stanley Hart White (1929)

Rubem Alves has written a small but beautiful book celebrating the incarnation and resurrection. It is called *I Believe in the Resurrection of the Body*. In it, Alves honors the body—both ours and God's in Jesus. As you read this passage from Alves' book, open yourself to experience these moments of prayer with your whole body, and with all your senses.

The Christians included a strange declaration in their Creed. They said they believed in and wished for the resurrection of the body. As if the body were the only thing of any importance.

But could there be anything more important? Could there be anything more beautiful?

It is like a garden, where flowers and
    fruits grow.
The smile grows there,
generosity,
compassion,
the will to struggle,
hope;
the desire to plant gardens,
to bear children,
to hold hands and stroll,
to know. . .
But the body is not only an overflow-
    ing spring: it is a welcoming lap.
The ear that hears the lament, in
    silence, without anything said.
The hand that grasps another. . .
The magical capacity to hear some-
    one's tears, far away, never seen,

and to weep also. . .
So simple, so lovely.

PRAY

Loving God, draw me near to you,
  body, mind, and heart.
Let me sit quietly in your presence
    so that I may hear with my own
      ears what you wish to say to
      me,
    so that I may feel with my
      own hands your closeness,
    so that I may see with my own
      eyes your love for me and for
      who I am.
Let me also come to understand,
    dear God,
  what it means to be a creature, a
    creation of yours
  from the top of my head to the end
    of my toes.
Let me rejoice in my body, in its
    strengths and its weakness,
  in its beauty and its usefulness,
  accepting my body, and myself,
    exactly as I am. Amen.

O World, I cannot hold
thee close enough.
  —Edna St. Vincent Millay

Suffering and Evil

"In moments of weakness and distress it is good to tread closely in God's footsteps."

—Aleksandr Solzhenitsyn

FOCUS

"The Lord rebuilds Jerusalem;
The Lord gathers in the exiles of
*   Israel.*
The Lord heals their shattered hearts
And binds up their wounds."

—Psalm 147:2-3, paraphrase

REFLECT

God is good.
God is just.
God is all-powerful.

You can reconcile any two of these, someone once said, but you cannot reconcile all three.

Evil, suffering, death. You don't have to have lived Job's life to understand how bad it can be—the unhelpable badness of the world. To call it overwhelming is to dishonor it by understatement.

What do you say to a parent whose child has died? What do you feel when you witness "ethnic cleansing" in Eastern Europe? What can you do as you look into the terrible face of the Holocaust, except to look away in horror? How do you face your own death?

You begin, perhaps, by facing it with rage and anger. You challenge God; you call God to account. The psalmist is not afraid to say it: "Why do You turn away? Why do You hide your face? Does the grave declare Your great love?"

This rage and questioning does not diminish God; quite the opposite—it takes God seriously. As Elie Wiesel says, "I do not have any answers, but I have some very good questions." Job is sure that God has deprived him of justice in his life, but he swears that as long as he is alive, he will not give up his faith in God.

Job stakes out a difficult position, one that generations of Jewish and Christian believers follow: Job will believe, but not without question. As Rabbi David Wolpe says, protest doesn't answer the question of evil, but it helps maintain the sanity of the accuser.

Inherent in our faith is another truth about suffering. While this truth does not answer the question of evil, it is a powerful companion to us in the midst of evil. It is the belief that no injustice in this world is suffered alone. No abuse is suffered alone. No evil is suffered alone. No death is suffered alone.

Where was God when the Jews were in the concentration camps on their way to the death chambers? God was in the camps on the way to the death chambers. God suffers with us. God weeps with us. God dies with us. God does this with all of us—not only for the good or righteous, but also for the very perpetrators of evil and death. The Midrashim of the rabbis tells of God's rebuke to the angels who began to sing a hymn of triumph as the sea drowned the Egyptians: "How can you sing," cries God, "while My creations are drowning?" (Sanhedrin 36b)

The suffering of God is powerful. It is vivid testimony to God's intimacy with us. It matters that when we suffer, we do not suffer alone. It matters very much.

But companionship is not a cure for pain, and God's suffering with us, as powerful as it is, cannot be an answer to the ravages of

How is faith to endure, O God, when you allow all this scraping and tearing on us? . . . If you have not abandoned us, explain yourself. We strain to hear. But instead of hearing answer we catch sight of God . . . scraped and torn. Through our tears we see the tears of God.
—Nicholas Wolterstorff, *Lament for a Son*

Some pains are too deep to salve and too inexplicably awful to pretend they have explanation.
—David J. Wolpe, *The Healer of Shattered Hearts*

The New Testament speaks of the Cross, part of whose meaning is that even out of the worst the world can do, God is still able to bring about the best. But all such explanations sound pale and inadequate before the gas chambers of Buchenwald and Ravensbruck, the ovens of Treblinka.

—Frederick Buechner, *Whistling in the Dark*

"I was consoling a little girl who was sick and had much pain," said Mother. "I told her. 'You should be happy that God sends you suffering, because your sufferings are a proof that God loves you much. Your sufferings are kisses from Jesus.' 'Then, Mother,' answered the little girl, 'please ask Jesus not to kiss me so much.' "

—Mother Teresa, in Edward Le Joly, *Mother Teresa of Calcutta*

evil. Ultimately, there is no answer that satisfies. Some are helpful. Some get us through one day to the next. But in the end, answers elude our grasp. The answer, Rabbi Yannai says, is not in our hands. In this life, that may be the last word: It is not in our hands.

So we continue to weep. We continue to rage. We continue to suffer with others. And we continue to pray.

ACT

The prayer following was found in German concentration camp archives and quoted in *Living Prayer* by Anthony Bloom. It is a powerful statement of grace in the middle of unspeakable suffering. Pray this prayer as a spiritual exercise for yourself in the next days.

PRAY

Peace to all men of evil will! Let there be an end to all vengeance, to all demands for punishment and retribution.... Crimes have surpassed all measure, they can no longer be grasped by human understanding. There are too many martyrs. . . . And so, weigh these sufferings not on the scales of thy justice, Lord, and lay not these sufferings to the torturor's charge to exact a terrible reckoning from them.

Pay them back in a different way! Put down in favor of the executioners, the informers, the traitors and all men of evil will, the courage, the spiritual strength of the others, their humility, their lofty dignity, their constant inner striving and invincible hope, the smile that staunched the tears, their love, their ravaged, broken hearts that remained steadfast and confident in the face of death itself, yes, even at the moments of the utmost weakness. . . .

Let all this, O Lord, be laid before thee for the forgiveness of sins, as a ransom for the triumph of righteousness, let the good and not the evil be taken into account! And may we remain in our enemies' memory not as their victims, not as a nightmare, not as haunting spectres, but as helpers in their striving to destroy the fury of their criminal passions. There is nothing more that we want of them.

—German concentration camp archives

The tears . . . streamed down, and I let them flow as freely as they would, making of them a pillow for my heart. On them it rested.

—Augustine, *Confessions IX, 12*

12

God's Graciousness

Grace Upon Grace

"Wake up to find out
that you are the eyes of the world."
> —Robert Hunter of the Grateful Dead, "Eyes of the World"

FOCUS

"Have you not known? Have you not heard? The Lord is the everlasting God, the Creator of the ends of the earth. [God] does not faint or grow weary; [God's] understanding is unsearchable. [God] gives power to the faint, and strengthens the powerless. Even youths will faint and be weary, and the young will fall exhausted; but those who wait for the Lord shall renew their strength, they shall mount up with wings like eagles, they shall run and not be weary, they shall walk and not faint."
> —Isaiah 40:28-31, paraphrase

REFLECT

"Marooned in mercy." That's how Ralph Wood describes grace. Grace is, he says, a comedy of redemption. To illustrate the point, Wood refers to the fiction of Peter De Vries, "a writer so funny," he says, "that it may seem inappropriate to take him seriously."

Puns (Like the cleaning lady, we all come to dust), aphorisms (What is an arsonist but someone who's failed to set the world on fire?), malapropisms (A novel should have a beginning, a muddle, and an end) and the surreal (A chiropractor treating a patient throws out his own back)—De Vries is master of all these and more.

Yet time and again De Vries's characters, in their own bumbling ways and in spite of their pessimistic philosophies, testify to divine grace set firmly in the muddle of human existence. As

Wood says, "[De Vries's] would-be atheists keep comically backsliding out of their unbelief, graciously lapsing into faith."

Maybe that's the way it is for us, too. Maybe God's grace—in Israel and in Christ—does negate our attempts to negate God's mercy. Perhaps we are daily "marooned in mercy," and marooned so thoroughly that we don't even recognize it—the way a fish is unaware of water or a bird of the wind that keeps it aloft. We are saved not by moralistic effort—there's no way to earn grace—but by unbidden grace. And that unbidden grace is near to hand, overhead and underfoot, in the eyes of strangers and friends, heard as laughter sometimes and sometimes as tears. Thank God for that.

ACT

Use the following daily examen, adapted from Ignatius of Loyola's *Spiritual Exercises*. This short prayer exercise is intended to increase your sensitivity to God's grace and God's Spirit working in your life.

At the end of the day, begin by looking back over the day and asking to see where you need to be thankful. Do not choose what you think you should be thankful for; instead, see what emerges, what you notice even slightly. Allow gratitude to take hold of you and express this to God.

The Puritans substituted a God who wished to damn people for a God who wished to save them.
—G. K. Chesterton, *Sidelights on New London and Newer New York*

Over the years, the encouragement and love of many people have sustained me in dark times, and these are debts which can never be fully repaid... mere gratitude is not enough.
—Tracy Thompson, *The Beast: A Reckoning with Depression*

Grace, thank God, is not dependent on our state of mind.

—Gerald G. May, *The Awakened Heart*

This is the crux of the matter. Either we expect to win life through our own efforts or else we recognize our incapacity and look only to grace.

—Paul Tournier, *A Doctor's Casebook in the Light of the Bible*

Next, ask for light to see what you need to understand about this day. Ask the Spirit to show you the different ways you have been graced today. Pause here to be in God's presence.

One more time, look over the events of the day. This time, ask God to show you where God's presence has been in your life—in you, in others, in the events of the world. Where and when do you sense the grace of God working? Is there any one area you are being nudged to focus on, to pray more deeply on, to take action on? Express to God what you need to express, and ask God for the grace to live tomorrow, with greater awareness of God's grace.

PRAY

The grace of God, deeper than our
   imagination;
the strength of Christ, stronger than
   our need;
and the communion of the Holy Spirit, richer than our togetherness;
guide and sustain us today and in all
   our tomorrows. Amen.

—Roger Knight, *The United Church of Christ Book of Worship*

The God Who Goes Before You

"And when the night is cloudy
There is still a light that shines on me."
—John Lennon and Paul McCartney,
"Let It Be"

FOCUS

"Where can I go from your spirit?
Or where can I flee from your presence?
If I ascend to heaven, you are there;
if I make my bed in Sheol, you are there.
If I take the wings of the morning
and settle at the farthest limits of the sea,
even there your hand shall lead me,
and your right hand shall hold me fast.
If I say, 'Surely the darkness shall cover me,
and the light around me become night,'
even the darkness is not dark to you;
the night is as bright as the day,
for darkness is as light to you."
—Psalm 139:7-12

REFLECT

My father died not long ago. He was a good man. I miss him more than I think I've yet realized. When I think of him—and I do, often—memories come flooding back.

In the late fifties, my family went to the local drive-in theater for entertainment. We'd all pile into the car (an old green Ford station wagon, excited about the prospects of popcorn and soft drinks. After we got to our parking spot, attached the tinny metal speaker to the car window, and adjusted the volume, everyone would settle in for a muggy, mosquito-filled evening of John Wayne or Doris Day.

On the way home, I'd inevitably fall asleep; and my dad would lift me out of the backseat, carry me into my room, put me in bed, and carefully tuck me in. Did my father know how warm, protected, and loved I felt as I drifted back off to sleep? Those nights are some of my fondest memories.

My father died, at age sixty-nine, of cancer. The disease slowly ate away at his body. The surgeries, radiation, and chemo treat-

Memory is a set of sagas we live by.

—Ivan Doig, *This House of Sky*

ments ravaged his body and his spirit. My once robust Coast Guard father weighed just 125 pounds at his death.

On my last visit to see him before his death, he insisted on being belted into the wheelchair, which he had been unable to get into for months, so that he could "sit at the table and have lunch with Tommy." He could barely eat—there was an oxygen tube in his nose—and he had trouble holding his head up, but he wanted to have lunch with me.

We were alone. We sat over lunch remembering stories from our life together and from his life before he became my father. It was a strong, intimate time for both of us. Then his energy began to falter, and he needed to rest. He asked me if I'd pick him up out of the wheelchair and take him back to his bed.

With great care I lifted him, carried him to the bed, and carefully tucked him in. As he slowly drifted to sleep, he kept telling me with great love how surprised he was that I could lift and carry him so easily. And I sat there beside him, remembering with tears the times when I was a child and he had carried me off to bed.

I miss my father. I do not know who will carry whom when we meet again. But I suppose in the end it does not matter, for God, I

THE LONG AND WINDING ROAD

am sure, will be there to carry us both.

God precedes us wherever we go. In his book *A Lover's Quarrel with the World*, Maurice Boyd writes of the celebrated English lay preacher Hugh Redwood. Redwood was facing a particularly difficult time in his life—a time when it seemed that no matter how earnestly he prayed, he felt the guidance of the Lord was far from him.

One night, while sitting beside a fire in the guest room where he was staying, Redwood happened to notice a Bible on the table beside his chair. The Bible was open to Psalm 59. Redwood began to read, and when he got to the tenth verse he found these words: "The God of my mercy shall prevent me."

The words Redwood read were from the King James Version of the Bible. To the modern reader, the word *prevent* means to keep something from happening. In 1611, in King James English, the word *prevent* meant *to go before.* Psalm 59:10 actually means, "The God of my mercy shall go before me."

After reading that psalm, Redwood noticed that someone had written in the margin a paraphrase that he would never forget: "My God, in loving kind-

To be hopeful, to embrace one possibility after another—that is surely the basic instinct. Baser even than hate, the thing with teeth, which can be stilled with a tone of voice or stunned by beauty. If the whole world of the living has to turn on the single point of remaining alive, that pointed endurance is the poetry of hope.

—Barbara Kingsolver, *High Tide in Tucson*

Life is truly a ride. We're all strapped in and no one can stop it. When the doctor slaps your behind, he's ripping your ticket and away you go. As you make each passage from youth to adulthood to maturity, sometimes you put your arms up and scream, sometimes you just hang on to that bar in front of you. But the ride is the thing. I think the most you can hope for at the end of life is that your hair's messed, you're out of breath, and you didn't throw up.

—Jerry Seinfeld, *SeinLanguage*

ness, goes before me at every corner." Powerful words. They spoke to Hugh Redwood that night. God was there. God's grace had preceded Redwood to that place, and God was waiting for him there.

In your prayer time, think about the many corners you have turned in your life. Remember the positive, nurturing ones. Remember, too, the devastating or draining ones. Take a moment to remind yourself that God, in loving-kindness, has promised to meet you at every corner.

PRAY

Amazing grace! How sweet the sound
    that saved a wretch like me!
I once was lost, but now am found;
    was blind, but now I see.

'Twas grace that taught my heart to
    fear, and grace my fears relieved;
how precious did that grace appear
    the hour I first believed.

Through many dangers, toils, and
    snares, I have already come;
'tis grace hath brought me safe thus
    far, and grace will lead me home.

The Lord has promised good to me,
    his word my hope secures;
he will my shield and portion be, as
    long as life endures.

Yea, when this flesh and heart shall
    fail, and mortal life shall cease,
I shall possess, within the veil, a life
    of joy and peace.

When we've been there ten thousand years, bright shining as the sun, we've no less days to sing God's praise than when we'd first begun.
—John Newton, 1779

I have seen flowers come
   in stony places
And kind things done by
   men with ugly faces,
And the gold cup won by
   the worst horse at the
   races,
So I trust, too.
—The Faber Book of Epigrams
and Epitaphs